TEN POTENT
PROOFS

FOR THE
PRETRIBULATION
RAPTURE

by

Lee W. Brainard

Soothkeep Press

The Bible version used in this work is the KJV modified with my own emendations in word order, modernization, and diction.

TABLE OF CONTENTS

Introduction

Satan is opposed to every institution of God. He hates Israel, the church, the Bible, the gospel, marriage, and the family. He hates the distinction between the sexes, eating meat and dairy, common sense, and every other good thing that God has given to man. He distorts every one of God's gifts, creating his own perverted versions of them. He fills the world with these lies, assailing men through the media, the educational system, the entertainment industry, the talking heads in the political arena, and the experts in the church world. Everywhere we turn, his foul breezes are blowing, and his lies are spreading.

One of the key prophetic institutions taught in the Bible is the pretribulation rapture. This teaching says that God will remove the church from Earth prior to the tribulation, the time of judgment that shall fall upon the world in the last days. This truth has not escaped the devil's scorn or his wiles. Because the Bible teaches it, he hates it.

Satan's favorite tactic with the pretrib rapture—his usual practice with all truth—is to smear and ridicule it. He bludgeons men with sound bites that demean it rather than convincing them with solid biblical arguments. "There is zero evidence for a pretrib rapture!" "No verse in the Bible teaches a pretribulation rapture!" "Dispensationalism is a manmade theological straightjacket that is forced upon the Bible!" "There are not two comings! The rapture and the second coming are the same thing!" "J.N. Darby invented the pretrib rapture!" "J.N. Darby got the pretrib rapture teaching from a false prophetess by the name of Margaret McDonald who got it from a deceiving spirit

7

pretending to be the Holy Spirit." "Why should the last generation of the church get a free pass from suffering and tribulation?" "Those who follow only the Bible and refuse to follow men never find the pretribulation rapture in the Bible."

But such claims are an ad hominem attack, not sound arguments. They boil down to an accusation of ignorance, of recklessness, of evading duty, of being mere followers of men. Only after potential converts are softened up by this emotional abuse, do the advocates of the post-tribulation rapture present their arguments—cherrypicked passages twisted to mean what God never intended to say. This tactic succeeds in convincing many that the pretrib rapture is a hoax foisted upon the church by deceivers who intentionally twist the scriptures.

The attacks have greatly increased in the past few decades, with an explosion of websites, YouTube channels, and other social media efforts maligning the pretrib rapture as a lie from hell. It is an interesting observation in psychology to note that the advocates of major error cannot be content to disagree. They feel compelled to slander pretribulationists as deceivers and false prophets.

Now, I do not believe in the pretrib rapture because I have never studied the other side and given it a fair hearing. This is far from the truth. I zealously adhered to a post-trib rapture for nearly a decade as a young Christian. I was convinced of this position for the same reason that many today believe in it. When I read Matthew 24, I saw saints gathered after the tribulation. I strengthened myself in this view by collecting and reading all the post-trib and anti-pretrib books that I could find. Inflamed by these volumes, I developed a rabid hatred for the pretrib rapture. This led to a harsh spirit that castigated my pretrib friends for being gullible, naïve, and ignorant.

But in the fall of 1989, after thousand of hours of research on the timing of the rapture over nine years, I experienced a sudden and forceful change. I had been trading letters with a preacher friend who was chipping away at my sticking points, and he made it abundantly clear from the Bible that the economy in the tribulation was the Jewish economy. The tribulation passages are focused on Messianic Jews who believe on Jesus and observe the Sabbath and the temple service. It dawned on me that I was guilty or overlooking (or ignoring) the Jewish context of Matthew 24 and other passages which address the tribulation of the last days.

So why do I now believe in a pretrib rapture? Because a robust examination of the evidence in the Bible, undertaken by an unprejudiced heart, points distinctly and conclusively to the truth of the pretribulation rapture.

In these pages I will present ten potent proofs that provide overwhelming evidence for the pretribulation rapture:

1. The Bible holds out a distinct future for Israel.

2. The Bible says that the 70th week is for Israel.

3. The Bible presents a temple-focused Israel in the tribulation, not the Christian church.

4. The Bible promises the church deliverance from the tribulation.

5. The Bible presents the church in heaven prior to the tribulation.

6. The Bible presents typologies of a pretribulation deliverance.

7. The Bible presents relative normality at the arrival of the day of the Son of man (the day of the Lord).

8. The Bible portrays the seals as visitations so distinct from mankind's normal troubles that they can only be the judgment at the end of the age.

9. The Bible makes a clear distinction between the rapture and the second coming.

10. The Bible presents the church as the body and bride of Christ.

PROOF 1

THE DISTINCT FUTURE OF ISRAEL

Israel's Rejection and Scattering

The Bible teaches that Israel was rejected by God because of her unbelief and iniquity. We see this in numerous passages. Two examples are Jeremiah 23:39 and Hosea 5:14.

> Behold, I, even I, will utterly forget you, and I will forsake you, and the city that I gave you and your fathers, and cast you out of my presence. (Jer. 23:39)

> For I will be unto Ephraim as a lion, and as a young lion to the house of Judah. I, even I, will tear and go away; I will take away, and none shall rescue him. (Hos. 5:14)

This rejection led to Israel being scattered among the nations, a painful discipline mentioned in many passages in the Old Testament. Deuteronomy 28:64 and Jeremiah 15:4 are prime examples.

> And the Lord shall scatter you among all people, from one end of Earth even unto the other; and there you shall serve other gods, which neither you nor your fathers have known, even wood and stone. (Deu 28:64)

> And I will cause them to be removed unto every kingdom on Earth because of Manasseh the son of Hezekiah king of Judah, for what he did in Jerusalem. (Jer 15:4)

But is this rejection and scattering permanent? Has God forsaken national Israel forever? Or is it temporary? Will God return to dealing with national Israel once again as his people and his testimony here on Earth?

A right understanding of this subject is critical if we would understand the Bible's eschatology and ecclesiology. Many folks have been led astray by the theory that Israel has been set aside permanently and not merely temporarily. They believe that God will never return to Israel as his earthly testimony. But God's return to Israel is a matter of God keeping his word and fulfilling his promises.

Promised Return

The rejection and scattering of Israel is a painful truth for the Jews, indeed for all who love God and his redemption. But Israel's sorrows over the past two thousand years are not the end of the story. God has promised to return to them. This is so clearly taught in the Bible that it is hard to believe that anyone can miss it. Hosea 3:4-5 and 5:15-6:2 are powerful testimonies to this truth.

> The children of Israel shall abide many days without king or prince, without sacrifice or sacred pillar, without ephod or teraphim. AFTERWARD, the children of Israel shall return and seek the Lord their God and David their king. They shall fear the Lord and his goodness in the latter days. (Hos.3:4-5)

> I will return again to my place UNTIL they acknowledge their offense. Then they will seek my face. In their affliction they will earnestly seek me. Come, and let us return to the Lord for he has torn, but he will heal us; he

has stricken, but he will bind us up. AFTER TWO DAYS he will revive us; ON THE THIRD DAY he will raise us up that we may live in his sight. (Hosea 5:15-6:2)

Consider the main points in the last passage:
1. The rejection of Israel. — *I will return to my place.*
2. Lasting hiatus — *Until they acknowledge their offense.*
3. Tribulation — *In their affliction, they will seek me.*
4. Repentance — *Come, let us return to the Lord.*
5. God's return — *After two days, he will raise us up.*

There is zero legitimate reason for doubt on this matter. God will once again embrace Israel as his earthly testimony. Her two thousand years of rejection will come to an end, and he will give the nation a second chance to nationally receive her Messiah and the new covenant in his blood. This is the only ground on which she can receive her Old Testament promises. And she will indeed receive her promises—all of them without fail.

What a God we serve! He extends undeserved grace to Jew and Gentile alike, no matter how long and how far they have fallen. He is the God of second chances.

Powerful Revival

God will give the nation of Israel a second chance in the tribulation. This time of trial, also known as the time of Jacob's trouble (Jer. 30:7), is designed to bring Israel to repentance and faith in their Messiah. This will indeed be the case as we read in Romans 11:26.

And so all Israel will be saved, as it is written: The Deliverer shall come out of Zion, and he shall turn away ungodliness from Jacob.

During the tribulation, the floodgates of salvation will be opened. Zechariah informs us that one-third of the nation will believe on the Lord and be saved (Zech. 13:9). This is a truly amazing statistic. In the midst of Israel's worst apostasy in her entire history, an outsized remnant will experience the mightiest revival of all time.

This outpouring of blessing will also flow out to the Gentiles in a way that is even more powerful than the blessing they received at the start of the church age. A clear testimony for this is found in Romans 11:12, 15.

> Now if their fall is riches for the world, and their failure
> riches for the Gentiles, how much more their fullness! ...
> For if their casting away was the reconciling of the world,
> what shall their reception be, but life from the dead?

How will this mighty work be carried out? Several factors will come into play. The Lord will pour out his Spirit upon all the believing Jews (Joel 2:28-31), and this blessing will likely spread to the Gentiles, according to the analogy in Acts. God will employ his 144,000 protected servants (Rev. 7:3-8). He will use the two witnesses (in my estimation Moses and Elijah) and their miracles to awaken many to the true biblical message. Finally, God will commission three angels, fluent in every tongue, who will circumnavigate the globe in the air to warn against Babylon, warn against the beast and his mark, and preach the everlasting gospel (Rev. 14:6-11).

Glorious Restoration

When the Lord purifies unto himself the nation of Israel and establishes his kingdom in their midst in Jerusalem, then he shall bless them as he has never blessed a nation before. He will

14

extend peace to her like a river and the glory of the nations like a flowing stream (Is. 66:12). Their ashes will be replaced with beauty and their mourning with the oil of joy (Is. 61:3). There will be water in the wilderness (Is. 35:6, 41:18-19), and the Dead Sea will be filled with fish (Ez. 47:8-12). They will enjoy the riches and glories of the Gentiles (Is. 61:6). Those nations and kingdoms that refuse to serve Israel will face severe judgment (Is. 60:12). Mt. Zion will be the joy of the whole globe (Ps. 48:2) and the perfection of beauty (Ps. 50:2). She will be covered by smoke by day and flaming fire by night (Is. 4:5), reminding the world that she enjoys the presence and protection of God.

Israel's Irrevocable Election

What is behind God's return to Israel? Sovereign election! This is taught all over the Bible. We read, for instance, in Deuteronomy 7:6:

> For you are a holy people to the Lord your God; the Lord your God has *chosen* you to be a people for himself, a special treasure above all the peoples on the face of Earth.

Despite the Bible's clarity on the point of Israel's election, many teachers insist that God set her aside permanently when she rejected and crucified her Messiah. But God vehemently denies the notion that he set Israel aside permanently and clarifies that her election still stands despite her rejection of her own Messiah and the promised new covenant. Consider the following statements found in Romans 11.

> All Israel will be saved ... concerning the gospel they are enemies for your sake, but concerning the election they are beloved for the sake of the fathers. (11:26-28)

15

> Has God cast away his people whom he foreknew? …
> Absolutely not! (11:2)

The truth is, God casting away those he has foreknown or elected is a theological impossibility. Romans 8:29-30 makes this point clear. All who participate in the first stage of God's redemption pipeline (foreknowledge) will, in due time, complete the last stage (glorification).

> For whom he foreknew, he also predestined … whom he predestined, these he also called; whom he called, these he also justified; and whom he justified, these he also glorified.

This is critical. God cannot foreknow and then unforeknow. He cannot choose and then unchoose. His choices are final and irrevocable. This is a theological constant. To challenge this point is to call into question his omniscience and integrity. He chose to make an unconditional covenant with Abraham to bless his descendants, the nation of Israel (Genesis 15). This election can no more be undone by her checkered past and present unbelief than our election can be undone by our past and present failures.

Given the clarity of the Bible on the subject, I find it perplexing that those who argue the loudest for unconditional, irrevocable election are often the same people who argue the hardest against the unconditional, irrevocable election of Israel.

So what is going on with Israel now? Paul explains in Romans 11:4-7 that a remnant is currently being saved during the church age while the nation as a whole is blinded.

> I have reserved to myself seven thousand men, who have not bowed the knee to Baal. Even so at this present time also there is a remnant according to the election of grace

16

... Israel has not obtained that which he seeks, but the election has obtained it, and the rest were blinded.

This remnant is the election of grace, not the election of Israel. It is the election of scattered individual Jews, not the election of national Israel. These are two different aspects of God's election.

But Israel's national blindness will not last forever. This is explained in verse 25, "blindness in part has happened to Israel UNTIL the fullness of the Gentiles be come in." Notice the word *until*. This implies that something stops and something else starts. When God's current plan with the Gentile church is completed, then he will turn to Israel, and remove the veil from her eyes, and wonderful things will happen.

But why is God going back to the nation that rejected the Messiah—indeed their own Messiah? Because he is God! He loves with an unfathomable ocean of love. He forgives with grace beyond human comprehension. He keeps his word and his promises (Tit. 2:28, Heb. 6:18). Paul lays this argument out in Romans 11:28-29.

As concerning the gospel, they are enemies for your sakes: but as touching the election, they are BELOVED for the fathers' sakes. FOR THE GIFTS AND CALLING OF GOD ARE WITHOUT REPENTANCE.

We often quote "for the gifts and calling of God are without repentance" with reference to our own situations, and applying this principle in this way is not wrong. But notice that this heartwarming truth is presented in reference to Israel's future restoration. God chose to introduce this vital insight on his immutability (unchangingness) with a pointed observation that he would not go back on the promises he made to Israel. He is committed absolutely to their restoration, and he will bring it to pass, humbling those quasi-evangelicals who hotly dispute it with their allegorizing methodologies.

"Beloved" means God's heart is in this return to the people and nation of Israel. Whether or not we can fit this into our theological conceptions is beside the point. It is a plain statement of scripture, and we are obligated to receive it and believe it. "Jacob have I loved, and Esau have I hated."

"Without repentance" means irrevocable. It means God cannot and will not change his mind on this matter. Why? Because his ways are pure and perfect. He makes no mistakes. There is never a need for him to change his plans. His plans are as immutable as he is. He has chosen Israel for definite purposes that concern a definite blessing in the definite future. These plans have not been permanently set aside or changed. They are still on track, and the day is fast approaching.

But when the Lord returns to Israel to bless them, this will not be so much for their sake as for his own. His name, his honor, and his word are at stake. This is clarified in Ezekiel 36:22 and its surrounding context.

> Thus says the Lord God, I do not do this for your sakes, O house of Israel, but for my holy name's sake, which you have profaned among the heathen, wherever you have gone.

Return to Israel Demands Pretrib Rapture

The fact that God will return to Israel demands a rapture before that time. James alluded to this when he addressed the church in Jerusalem in Acts 15:14-16. At this convocation, Peter had earlier explained how God had used him to bring the gospel to the Gentiles for the first time. Then Paul and Barnabas declared to the church in Jerusalem how God had worked wonders among the Gentiles through them. When they were done with their testimony, James spoke up and said:

> Simeon has declared how God FIRST VISITED THE GENTILES, to take out of them a people for his name. And to this agree the words of the prophets; as it is written, AFTER THIS I will return, and will build again the tabernacle of David, which is fallen down; and I will build again its ruins, and I will set it up.

Some get confused here and equate the Lord visiting the Gentiles with the Lord rebuilding the tabernacle of David. This is a mistake. James was not spiritualizing the temple. He was not equating the gathering of the Gentiles and the building of the temple. He was distinguishing them.

Notice that James says, *"after this."* God doesn't return to Israel and rebuild the temple until *after* he has finished gathering a people from the Gentiles. This informs us that the church age will come to its conclusion first, and then the Lord will return to Israel, favor Jerusalem, and rebuild the temple.

How did James figure out this order? He put two and two together. He knew that God had foretold his long and painful rejection of Israel and his ultimate return to her. He saw this in such passages as Hosea 5:14-6:2 and Amos 9:9-11. He knew that the scriptures held out the promise that all nations would be blessed through Abraham's seed (Gen. 18:18). He knew that the Lord's name would be praised from the rising of the sun to its going down (Ps. 113:3). He had heard the great commission from the Lord's lips exhorting his followers to take the gospel message to every nation (Matt. 28:19-20). He had seen and heard about the Lord's work among the Gentiles from the lips of his fellow apostles. He knew there was no way under the sun that the Lord was going to sit on his hands or twiddle his thumbs, more or less doing nothing here on Earth, between his rejection of Israel and his restoration of Israel. He concluded from all this that God's current efforts in gathering Gentiles unto himself were the fulfillment of the promised blessing for the Gentiles through Abraham's seed. A current Gentile church program dovetailed perfectly with the Lord's rejection of Israel, his long hiatus away from them, and his last-days return to his people.

So how does Israel's prophesied future restoration point to a pretribulation rapture? Because the Lord cannot have two distinct testimonies on Earth at the same time. If the Lord is going to return to Israel as his testimony, then the time of the church as his testimony must come to an end. This is exactly what we see in the pages of scripture. We see God returning to Israel after he has finished gathering his Gentile church. We see God dealing with Israel during the tribulation. Therefore, we conclude that the church must be raptured before the tribulation.

PROOF 2

THE SEVENTIETH WEEK
APPOINTED FOR ISRAEL

God on the Seventieth Week

There is much speculation on the purpose of the seventieth week, popularly known as the tribulation. There is no need for this speculation. God has plainly told us what his purposes are for the seventieth week in Daniel 9:24, a passage that is critical for understanding prophecy. Here we read:

> Seventy weeks are determined upon YOUR PEOPLE and upon YOUR HOLY CITY to finish the transgression, to make an end of sins, to make reconciliation for iniquity, to bring in everlasting righteousness, to seal up the vision and prophecy, and to anoint the most Holy [the temple].

If we consistently follow literal interpretation when we study this passage, then the purpose of the seventieth week—*who* God is working with and *what* he wants to accomplish—becomes as clear as the noon day sun. God is focusing on Israel. His purpose is to address Israel's problem with sin and unbelief. This is made clear by the three main components of the passage—the parties, the purpose, and the parenthesis.

The parties. Seventy weeks were declared upon Daniel's people and Daniel's holy city. Daniel was a Jew (Dan. 1:6-7), and he prayed toward Jerusalem (Dan. 6:10), the holy city of the

Jews. The phrase *your people*, therefore, can only refer to Israel. And the phrase *your holy city*, likewise, can only refer to Jerusalem. This information tells us exactly what God's purpose will be in the seventieth week. SINCE God declared the seventy weeks upon Israel and Jerusalem, and SINCE God's focus during the first sixty-nine weeks was upon Israel and Jerusalem, THEN God's focus during the seventieth week must be upon Israel and Jerusalem in the same way.

The purpose. The purpose here is not Christ's atoning work on the cross, nor his work in reconciling the Gentiles to God. God tells us what his purpose is: dealing with Israel's sin and transgression, addressing her iniquity, reconciling the nation to himself, bringing them to permanent right living and thinking, bringing vision and prophecy to a permanent end (because the Messiah will be on Earth in person), and anointing the temple. This boils down to a full restoration of the nation. Now this restoration will come through the new covenant in Christ and his blood. That is a certainty. The Jews must believe on Jesus as the Messiah, or they will never be restored to fellowship with God and will never receive their Old Testament promises: kingdom, temple, and throne.

SINCE these purposes were the purpose of the seventy weeks, and SINCE they were not fulfilled literally in Israel and Jerusalem during the first sixty-nine weeks, and they have not been fulfilled literally in Israel and Jerusalem in the interim, THEN we are forced to conclude that they must be fulfilled literally in Israel and Jerusalem during a yet future seventieth week.

The parenthesis. This passage concerns four hundred and ninety years (seventy weeks of years) that were declared upon the nation of Israel. The context reveals that four hundred and eighty-three years (sixty-nine weeks) were completed when the

Messiah was crucified (Dan. 9:26) and that the final week of years (the seventieth week) was still future when Jerusalem fell in AD 70 (Dan. 9:27). This demands a parenthesis between the sixty-ninth and seventieth week—a time when the Lord is departed from Israel as his people. This time of separation has now stretched out for more than nineteen painful centuries for Israel.

Now the dark cloud of the parenthesis comes with a silver lining of restoration. The end of the parenthesis is just as certain as the fact of the parenthesis. God must and will return to Israel to finish his work with her. His declaration regarding the seventy weeks is immutable. And so is every other statement in the Bible on the rejection and restoration of Israel. "My word shall not return to me void" (Is. 55:11). God kept his word regarding the first sixty-nine weeks in every detail. He will keep his word regarding the seventieth week in every detail.

But the context also reveals that God's return to dealing with Israel doesn't start with blessing. The seventieth week starts with the antichrist forcing a treaty with Sheol upon the nation as a whole[1] (Dan. 9:27, Is. 28:18). There is moral congruity here. The sixty-ninth week ended with Israel rejecting the true Messiah. The seventieth will start with Israel accepting the false messiah. God will pick up with Israel right where he left off with her on her trajectory of unbelief, aiming to turn her from the weakness and emptiness of the law and bring her into the blessings of the Messiah and the new covenant in his blood. This is a return to the scene of failure to offer the nation a second chance. There will be a door of hope in the valley of Achor (Hos. 2:15).

The Time of Jacob's Trouble

Daniel 9:24 clearly states that the tribulation (the final seven years of the age) will be upon Israel. We find the same thought expressed in Jeremiah 30:7. "Alas! for that day is great, so that none is like it: it is the time of Jacob's trouble, but he shall be saved out of it."

There is nothing difficult to understand here. *Jacob* refers to all of the descendants of Jacob. It is another term for the Jews. The *time of Jacob's trouble* is the time of great tribulation for the Jews at the end of the age. It will be the worst persecution that any nation on Earth has ever experienced in the entire history of the world (Matt. 24:21). The persecution of the Jews under Adolf Hitler will pale in comparison. It is estimated that one-third of the Jews perished at the hands of that cruel monster. Zechariah 13:8-9 informs us that two-thirds of the nation shall be cut off and killed during the tribulation. But one-third will be brought through the fire and be refined as silver and gold are refined.

Daniel 12:1 also makes reference to this great tribulation at the end of the age.

> At that time Michael shall stand up, the great prince who stands watch over the sons of your people. And there shall be a time of trouble, such as never was since there was a nation, even to that time. And at that time your people shall be delivered, every one who is found written in the book.

Once again, the time of awful tribulation at the end of the age has Israel as its focus. But the Jews will not be on their own. The same God who provides the tribulation for their purging will also provide protection and help. They will not be tested beyond what they are able. God has appointed the archangel Michael to be their chief guardian when they pass through the fire of the great tribulation.

One other thing should be pointed out. This awful hour is not merely the antichrist and the nations turning their ungodly hands against Israel. This is not merely man's wrath against the people and things of God. This is the refining fire of God. God shall turn his hand against his sheep (Zech. 13:7) and stretch out his hand against Judah and Jerusalem (Zeph. 1:4). Behind the apparent madness of this fiery trial there is glorious rhyme and reason. Jeremiah 30:8-9 informs us that this trial is designed to break the yoke of bondage off Israel's neck and bring the long recalcitrant nation to repentance that she might serve the Lord her God (Jesus the Messiah) and David her king. This goes along with the divine purpose stated in Daniel 9:24: fix Israel's unbelief problem and anoint the millennial temple. What a glorious day that will be!

The Holy Place and the Abomination

Matthew 24:15-21, one of the most well-known passages on the tribulation in the Bible, clearly associates the tribulation with Israel and with a temple in Jerusalem that God owns as his holy place. Here we read:

> WHEN you see the abomination of desolation spoken of by Daniel the prophet standing in the holy place (whoever reads, let him understand), THEN let those who are in Judea flee to the mountains … For THEN there will be great tribulation, such as has not been since the beginning of the world until this time, nor ever shall be.

Several clues in this passage demonstrate the focus on Israel. The antichrist will plant his ungodly feet in the holy place, which is undeniably a reference to the physical temple in Jerusalem.

25

The inhabitants of Israel[2] are warned to flee when this vile man stands in the temple. The flight is to the mountains, which can only be the nearby mountains of the Judean wilderness or the Jordanian Highlands. The antichrist's foray into the temple will inaugurate a time of horrible persecution for the Jews, which will transcend every prior tribulation that any nation has ever faced in the history of the world. The focus in this passage is so clearly Israel that a man would have to be intentionally blind to miss it. Nothing here is addressed to the inhabitants of Montana or New York or France or England.

Notice further that the Bible calls the temple in Jerusalem "the holy place." Not "your temple." Not "your holy place." But simply "the holy place" without qualification. This implies that it actually is holy in God's eyes during the seventieth week, the same way that it was holy in his eyes during the first sixty-nine weeks. God owns the temple. This is a return to the state of things prior to the cross and the rending of the vail.

It should also be pointed out that the antichrist's foul deed is called *the abomination of desolation* because the temple actually is the temple of God. Were it merely honored by men as the temple of God, it would be sacrilegious to defile it in man's eyes, but it would not be abomination in God's eyes. It is abomination because God owns the temple, and his name is on that piece of real estate. He does not own it for what the Jews have made of it, but for his own redemption purposes and plans.

Now God owning the temple is contrary to the church age. The church age is a heavenly (or pilgrim) economy. During this time the testimony of God is not attached to any particular piece of real estate or holy place. There is no physical temple. Instead, the church is a spiritual temple. Throughout the last age, the Mosaic dispensation, the temple was THE house of God. God's name was fixed there (Deut. 12:5). Even during Christ's earthly ministry, he referred to the temple as "my Father's house."

But shortly before the cross, at the tail end of the sixty-ninth week, as things geared up for the church age, he said to Israel, "Your house is left to you desolate." This was a divine rejection of the temple. As the Shekinah, the physical presence of God, had already departed (Ezek. 10), so now the providential presence of God would depart. This was typified at the cross when the massive vail was rent from top to bottom (Matt. 27:51). God set aside the physical temple as his testimony on Earth so he could take up the spiritual temple as his testimony down here

At the end of the church age, the reverse transaction has to occur. As the Lord rent the vail in the earthly temple, thus setting it aside, before he started building the heavenly temple at the feast of Pentecost, so he must remove the heavenly temple from Earth in the rapture before he can return to the physical temple and the last seven years of the Mosaic dispensation.

Jewish Focus Demands Pretrib Rapture

The scriptures are clear that during the seventieth week, commonly known as the tribulation, God's focus will be on the people and nation of Israel as his people, on Jerusalem as his holy city, and on the rebuilt temple as his holy place. Indeed, he declared that the seventy weeks were upon Israel and Jerusalem to bring them to repentance and faith. And he calls the tribulation the time of Jacob's trouble.

At this point, logic should kick in and do its thing. God can't have two honored economies running at the same time. IF we see that God has returned to Israel and Jerusalem as his program during the tribulation, THEN we are forced to conclude that the church isn't here on Earth during the tribulation. She has already been taken to heaven in the rapture.

The same point can be made from a slightly different angle. God can't have two honored temples on Earth at the same time. IF we see that the physical temple in Jerusalem is the temple of God on Earth during the tribulation, THEN we are forced to conclude that the spiritual temple of the church can't be on Earth during the tribulation. She has already been taken to heaven in the rapture.

PROOF 3

ISRAEL IN THE TRIBULATION

Saints in the Tribulation

The scriptures plainly present saints in the tribulation. There is zero room for disputing this. In Matthew 24:31 the Lord gathers his elect from around the world who have survived the tribulation. In Revelation 12:14 a Jewish remnant flees to a hiding place in the wilderness. In Revelation 13:4 the antichrist makes war against the saints. And in Revelation 7:9-17, we see a great multitude coming out of the tribulation, a multitude so great that no man can number it. They come from every nation, tribe, people, and language.

Personally, I believe that there will be a great revival in the tribulation, at least during the first half. This will be brought about by various causes including the shock of the rapture, the hundred and forty-four thousand, the two witnesses, the three angels who speak from heaven, and the outpouring of the Holy Spirit like at Pentecost, who will present the new covenant blessings in the Messiah with a powerful work that convicts men of sin, righteousness, and judgment to come. The supernatural manifestations of the Lord on behalf of the gospel during the tribulation will far surpass anything seen in this age.

Christians or Tribulation Saints?

The presence of believers in the tribulation raises a big question. Who are they? Are they Christians? Many insist that they must be Christians because they believe in Jesus. But the definition of Christian requires some clarification. What do we mean by Christian?

Obviously, the tribulation saints are Christians, if by this term we simply mean that they have believed in the Lord Jesus as the only way of salvation. No one in this age or the next can be saved apart from faith in Jesus. As we read, "Neither is there salvation in any other for there is no other name under heaven given among men, whereby we must be saved" (Acts 4:12). The tribulation saints are under no less obligation to believe in Jesus than the saints of the present church age.

But using the title *Christian* for the saints in the tribulation is misleading because they will observe the law as well as trust in Jesus. They will be obligated to the Sabbath (Matt. 24:20). They will worship in the temple, and their worship will be accepted by God (Rev. 11:1). They will sing the song of Moses as well as the song of the Lamb (Rev. 15:3). This is contrary to the Christianity of the present age. Christians don't observe the law or keep the Sabbath. Such things are not part of our testimony.

Because of these differences, the label *Messianic Jews*— that is, Jews who believe on Jesus as their promised Messiah and keep the law—much better describes the tribulation saints than does the label *Christians*. Christians and Messianic Jews share the same redemption—the same Saviour, the same new birth, the same gospel, and the same new covenant—but they have a very different outward form of religion. The Jews have a heavy religious yoke of ceremonies and laws (Acts 15:10). Christians have no such yoke. Our forms are minimal. We were given baptism, the Lord's table, and a little information on the structure of the church.

It will help to clarify the difference between the tribulation saints and the church-age saints if we can wrap our minds around the difference between the disciples before the cross and the disciples after Pentecost. During the time of Jesus' sojourn, the disciples were Christians in the sense that they believed on him as the Messiah. But they were not Christians in the sense of belonging to the universal church. How so? Because that glorious institution did not yet exist. It was still future according to the Lord's explicit statement, "On this rock I SHALL build my church" (Matt. 16:18). It did not pass from the realm of prophecy to the realm of reality until the first Pentecost after Christ's death on the cross.

Moreover, the Lord's disciples prior to the cross were not Christians in the sense of embracing only the distinct practices of Christianity. They still adhered to the formalities of Judaism. The distinct practices of Christianity were not introduced until after the Jerusalem council had recognized that God was doing something new with the Gentiles (Acts 15) and the apostles had received the mystery of the church (Eph. 3:2-6).

Now the saints in the tribulation (the seventieth week) will be on the same ground that the disciples were in the time of Christ's sojourn (the sixty-ninth week). They will be believers in Jesus as the Messiah, but they will also be obligated to the law as the God-given outward religion. This obligation to the law for the duration of the seventy weeks is what the Lord intended to convey with his exhortation in Matthew 5:17-19.

Do not think that I am come to destroy the law and the prophets. I am not come to destroy but fulfill. For verily I say unto you, until heaven and Earth pass, not one jot or tittle shall pass from the law in any way, until all be fulfilled. Whoever breaks the least of these commandments will be the least in the kingdom.

If you attempt to apply this obligation to the law in the current age, you are forced to make a figurative application of it that excludes the law proper and includes only the new covenant teachings that supersede the law. But if you apply this obligation to the law in the sixty-ninth week (Christ's earthly ministry) and in the seventieth week (the tribulation), when the disciples will be obliged to both believe on Jesus and keep the law, then this passage can enjoy a strictly literal fulfillment.

The Law Doesn't Replace the Gospel

Two clarifications need to be made when it comes to the obligation to the law during the tribulation. *First of all,* the return to the Mosaic law during the tribulation is a matter of outward testimony, not a change in the salvation plan. As Paul informs us, "By the deeds of the law no flesh shall be justified in his sight, for by the law is the knowledge of sin" (Rom. 3:20). This is not a truth statement applicable only to the church age. This is a timeless truth. Nobody ever has or ever will be saved by the law, including the tribulation saints. They will be saved *under* the law (the law as the established outward religious form). They will not be saved *by* or *through* the law. This is a vital distinction. The Mosaic law will be the external context of salvation not the ground or condition of salvation.

Secondly, the return to the Mosaic law during the tribulation is neither a reversal nor a compromise of policy. It is a matter of God taking care of unfinished business with the nation of Israel. He is returning to the people under the law to give them a second chance to embrace the new covenant in Jesus' blood. When he resumes dealing with Israel shortly before the seventieth week, he will pick up with them right where he left off after the sixty-ninth week—the nation in the grip of a profound unbelief that had rejected their Messiah despite the profuse light given to them and had twisted the scriptures into a system of dead traditions.

Identifying the Tribulation Saints

No passage in the New Testament that presents saints in the tribulation offers any information that positively identifies them as church-age Christians. On the contrary, every passage that presents the distinctive features of these believers presents them laboring under the Mosaic economy. This indicates that the God-ordained economy during the tribulation will be the Mosaic law and that the "Christians" will be Messianic Jews, not church age-Christians. Consider the following lines of evidence which prove this point.

The temple and the sabbath. Matthew 24:15-21 presents some of the most compelling testimony in the New Testament that the seventieth week will feature the Mosaic economy.

> When you see the abomination of desolation … standing in THE HOLY PLACE (the temple), then let those who are in Judea flee to the mountains … pray that your flight be not on the SABBATH … For then there will be great tribulation.

Notice that the temple is called *the holy place*. This agrees with 2 Thessalonians 2:4 and Revelation 11:1 where it is called *the temple of God* and with Malachi 3:1 where we read that the Messiah will come to *his temple*. Such statements do not merely present man's opinion of the tribulation temple. They present

God's opinion of it. He owns the temple in Jerusalem as his holy place. This is contrary to the church age. There is no physical temple in the church age. We *are* the temple.

Notice further the premium placed on keeping the *sabbath*. This is not man thinking that he is subject to the sabbath. This is God reminding the saints that they are obligated to the sabbath. This is contrary to the church age. The church is not obligated to the sabbath. The church is dead to the law.

The song of Moses and the song of the Lamb. Another compelling testimony on the economy of the seventieth week is found in Revelation 15:2-3.

> And I saw as it were a sea of glass mingled with fire: and them that had gotten the victory over the beast, and over his image, and over his mark, and over the number of his name, stand on the sea of glass, having the harps of God. And they sing THE SONG OF MOSES the servant of God, and THE SONG OF THE LAMB, saying, Great and marvelous are your works, Lord God Almighty; just and true are your ways, O King of saints.

Notice that those singing these two songs together are not well-meaning but misguided believers down here on Earth. They are tribulation martyrs standing on the sea of glass in the presence of God Almighty. This implies that God approves of their song selection. It also implies that the economy during the tribulation involves a return to the Mosaic law. If the economy of the tribulation were the Christianity of the present age, the martyrs wouldn't be singing the song of Moses. How could they? Christians are dead to the law (Rom. 7:4).

The temple, altar, and worshippers. In Revelation 11:1-2 we yet find another temple-based piece of evidence that the saints in the tribulation are Messianic Jews and not church-age Christians.

> Then I was given a reed like a measuring rod. The angel stood, saying, rise and measure THE TEMPLE OF GOD, THE ALTAR, and THOSE WHO WORSHIP THERE. But leave out the court which is outside the temple, and do not measure it, for it has been given to the Gentiles. They will tread the holy city underfoot for forty-two months.

Here we find the Lord sending one of his angels to measure not only the temple and altar, but also those that worship there. This effort isn't to satisfy curiosity or provide confirmation. God is omniscient. He already knows the dimensions of the temple and the altar. He already knows how many Jews are worshiping in the temple precincts. This effort portrays God owning the temple, accepting temple worship (not as an end in itself but for what it represents), and accepting the temple worshippers. This is contrary to the Christianity of the present age. There is no physical temple in the present age, and Christians do not engage in physical temple worship.

Mosaic law in the seventieth week. Now the seventieth week featuring the Mosaic law makes sense when we grasp the relationship between the seventieth week and the sixty-ninth week. Bear in mind that the seventy weeks were declared upon Israel and Jerusalem as a unified block of time with a unified purpose (Dan. 9:24-27). This implies that God's relationship with Israel and Jerusalem during the seventieth week (the tribulation) will be the same as it was during the sixty-ninth week (the Lord's sojourn). Since the temple in Jerusalem was regarded as God's house in the sixty-ninth week (John 2:16), it must also be the house of God in the seventieth week. It would be inconsistent if the temple were the house of God during the sixty-nine weeks and a disowned facade during the seventieth week.

These four observations demonstrate beyond all shadow of doubt that the tribulation saints will be obligated by God to both observe the Mosaic law and believe on Jesus. This necessitates a pretribulation rapture. The Lord cannot return to requiring the law until he has ended the church program and removed the church from the Earth.

The Two Witnesses

My favorite passage for presenting the distinction between the tribulation and the church age is Revelation 11:3-6. Here we see the two witnesses calling down fire and plagues from heaven.

> I will give power to my two witnesses, and they will prophesy one thousand two hundred and sixty days, clothed in sackcloth … If anyone wants to harm them, FIRE PROCEEDS FROM THEIR MOUTHS and devours their enemies. If anyone wants to harm them, he must be killed in the same manner. They have POWER TO SHUT HEAVEN, so that no rain falls in the days of their prophesying; and they have POWER OVER THE WATERS to turn them to blood, and [POWER] TO STRIKE EARTH with all plagues, as often as they desire.

Such activity is contrary to the church age. No such activity is taught, encouraged, or exampled in the New Testament. On the contrary, notice how the Lord responded to his disciples in Luke 9:52-56 when they wanted to engage in this kind of activity and call down fire from heaven upon the unbelieving Samaritans.

They entered a village of the Samaritans … But they did not receive him … When his disciples James and John saw this, they said, Lord, do you want us to command fire to come down from heaven and consume them, like Elijah did? He turned and rebuked them, and said, YOU DON'T KNOW WHAT KIND OF SPIRIT YOU ARE. For the Son of man did not come to destroy men's lives but to save them.

Notice that when James and John wanted to call down fire from heaven, the Lord rebuked them and said, "You don't know what kind of spirit you are." He wasn't rebuking them for ungodliness or lack of salvation. He was admonishing them for being stuck in the Mosaic economy. They didn't get what the Lord was trying to do. They didn't understand that he was in the process of changing dispensations, and that they needed to leave the old economy behind, where calling down fire from heaven was legit, and get on board with the new economy where this practice was absent.

The Tribulation Saints and the Rapture

Everywhere we look in the Bible, the saints we see in the tribulation are Jewish believers in the Messiah who serve God through the Mosaic law with a particular focus on the temple service. We don't see church-age Christianity or church-age Christians anywhere. This forces unprejudiced students of the Bible to conclude that the tribulation believers are Messianic Jews and not church-age Christians. This, in turn, implies that the church age has concluded and that the church has been removed from Earth before the tribulation.

PROOF 4

DELIVERANCE FROM WRATH

Not Appointed to Wrath

One of the strongest arguments for a pretribulation rapture is the promise that the church will not see the wrath of God that is coming upon the world at the end of the age. This promise is clearly stated in 1 Thessalonians 1:10 and 5:9-10.

To wait for his Son from heaven, whom he raised from the dead, even Jesus who delivers us from the WRATH to come. (1 Thess. 1:10)

For God has not appointed us to WRATH, but to obtain salvation by our Lord Jesus Christ, who died for us, that, whether we wake or sleep, we should live together with him. (1 Thess. 5:9)

Some, however, insist that *wrath* in these verses refers to eternal judgment, not to the time of temporal judgment that falls upon the world in the last days. In other words, they regard these verses as references to soteriological wrath in the lake of fire, not eschatological wrath poured out on Earth. But they are mistaken. Consider the following three points.

First of all, when the Bible presents eternal wrath in the lake of fire, it does so with contextual clues such as mentions of fire, gehenna, outer darkness, eternal torment, eternal punishment, and wailing and gnashing of teeth. Such clues are lacking in the context of the two verses cited above. A helpful rule of thumb is that generic terms like *wrath* and *judgment* should be regarded as eschatological judgment that falls upon the world at the end of the age unless something in the context distinctly indicates that the focus is eternal judgment in the lake of fire.

Secondly, these promises of deliverance from the coming wrath can't be references to eternal wrath because Christians are already delivered from that awful reality. Our deliverance from eternal punishment is a historical fact, not a future event. The moment we were born again, we were transferred from the broad road that leads to destruction to the narrow road that leads to life. The promises of deliverance from wrath, therefore, can only refer to the church's deliverance from the wrath that the Lord will pour out upon the world at the end of the age.

Thirdly, both of these verses involve a separation of mankind before the wrath is poured out on Earth. In 1 Thessalonians 1:10, Jesus comes for his church before the wrath arrives and delivers her before it falls. We go up, the wrath comes down.

In 1 Thessalonians 5:9-10, the church's deliverance from wrath is associated with the resurrection. In one moment every believer on the entire planet, whether sleeping (dead) or awake (alive), will experience two amazing changes. They will be transformed to bear the likeness of Jesus, and they will be transferred to heaven to dwell with him. This heavenly transfer is the mechanism that will deliver the living saints from the wrath to come. What a precious promise this is for those who long for the Lord's coming! But those who are not born again will be left behind to endure the wrath that shall engulf the entire planet.

Once we consider the context and theological connections of the deliverance-from-wrath verses, it becomes obvious that they are promises that we shall not see the wrath that God shall pour out at the end of the age. This is a pretribulation rapture.

Are Tribulation and Wrath Distinct?

Historically, those who employ literal interpretation have almost universally regarded the promise of removal before wrath as a promise of removal before the seventieth week. They regarded the terms *wrath*, *judgment*, and *tribulation* as synonyms that all referred to the seventieth week though they differed in nuance. The seventieth week was God-imposed tribulation, God-imposed wrath, and God-imposed judgment.

In recent years, prophecy teachers who hold the so-called prewrath rapture position have found fault with this handling. They insist that tribulation and wrath are mutually exclusive concepts that have zero overlap. Consequently, they regard it as absurd for pretribulationists to confuse them and employ them both as labels for the seventieth week.

The way they see it, *tribulation* refers only to man's efforts against man, while *wrath* refers to God's righteous judgments upon the world. The church has no promise of deliverance from tribulation, not even that under the antichrist. Her only promise of deliverance is that she will be spared from God's wrath. This forces them to embrace a unique handling of the seventieth week. They regard the first six to six-and-a-half years as tribulation under the antichrist and only the short remainder as God's wrath. The church will endure the tribulation and be raptured prior to the small window of wrath.

Tribulation Used for the Wrath of God

The idea that tribulation and wrath do not overlap, while it sounds plausible at first, is a mistake. Those who allow the Bible to trump gee-whiz theories will observe that the Bible employs these terms interchangeably for the time of visitation at the end of the age. Consider the following passages where *tribulation* is used for the time of wrath.

Paul uses *tribulation* as a description of the day of wrath. In Romans 2:5-9 Paul describes the coming judgment of God upon the world as "the day of *wrath* and the revelation of the righteous judgment of God" when the whole of mankind shall face "indignation and *wrath*, TRIBULATION and anguish."

The Septuagint uses *tribulation* as a description of the day of the Lord. In Zephaniah 1:14-17 the day of Armageddon is described as a *day of wrath* and a *day of tribulation.*

> The great day of the Lord is near, it is near and hastes greatly, even the sound of the day of the Lord. The mighty man shall cry there bitterly. That day is a *day of wrath*, a *day of* TRIBULATION and distress, a day of devastation and desolation, a day of darkness and gloominess, a day of clouds and thick darkness ... And I will bring distress upon men, that they shall walk like blind men, because they have sinned against the Lord, and their blood shall be poured out as dust, and their flesh as dung.

In Habakkuk 3:12-16 we find another instance where the day of Armageddon is described as a time of *wrath* (indignation, anger) and a day of *tribulation.*

> You marched through the land in *indignation.* You trampled the nations in *anger.* You went forth for the salvation of your people [Israel], for salvation with your Anointed. You struck the head of the house of the wicked [the antichrist] ... You walked through the sea with your horses, through the heap of great waters. When I heard, my body trembled; My lips quivered at the voice ... And

I trembled in myself, that I might rest in the day of TRIBULATION. When he comes up unto the people, he will invade them with his troops.

Now the fact that the Bible uses *tribulation* as a description for Armageddon is telling. No one doubts that this day is the final day of the seventieth week. No one doubts that this day is the great day of the Lord, when the world faces judgment and wrath of the severest degree, without admixture of grace. This forces us to a sweeping conclusion. IF tribulation legitimately covers the worst degrees of wrath, THEN it legitimately covers the entire spectrum of wrath.

Wrath Used for the Tribulation

Not only does the Bible use *tribulation* for the day of the Lord, but it also uses *wrath* for the great tribulation under the antichrist. Luke 21:21-23 refers to this persecution of the Jews as "the days of VENGEANCE" and "WRATH upon this people." This is God's wrath under consideration, not Satan's. It is God putting Israel in the pressure cooker of judgment and affliction, also called the time of Jacob's trouble (Jer. 30:7), so that the nation will repent and believe in her own Messiah (Hos. 5:15).

In the same spirit, 2 Thessalonians 2 presents two bits of information that identify the antichrist as a judgment from God. The first is the observation that the antichrist is a delusion sent by God to deceive the ungodly that they might be condemned (vv. 8-12). The second is the observation that the revelation of the antichrist is THE proof that mankind is in the day of the Lord (vv. 2-3). Did you catch that? The entire time of the antichrist, which we commonly call the tribulation, is the dawning of the day of the Lord.

This information forces us to an inescapable conclusion: IF the time of the antichrist is the day of the Lord, and IF the antichrist is a delusion sent by God as a judgment for unbelief, and IF the time of the antichrist is vengeance and wrath from God, THEN the time of tribulation under the antichrist is last-days wrath. How can any man squirm out of this?

Wrath Comes in Degrees

One of the reasons that men struggle with the question of when the wrath of God starts in the last days is that they have embraced the mistaken idea that God's wrath is a monolithic block of time that doesn't feature degrees or increases. It starts full blast and continues full blast. But this is a mistake.

You will have a difficult time picturing the correct outline of the last days if you don't understand that the wrath of God poured out on the world in the last days comes in degrees. This is illustrated by the Bible's presentation of the day of the Lord. As a literal day has stages, so the day of the Lord has stages. It *starts* with the morning star (the rapture), which is the early warning sign of the approaching day, *advances* with the dawning of the day (the tribulation), and *arrives* with the sunrise (the second coming). The *day proper* is the thousand years, which is the Lord's day in contrast to man's day.

Why is this important to understand? Because the church is not merely promised deliverance from the day of the Lord in its severest degrees, but from the entire spectrum—dawning to sunrise. How do we know this? From two considerations. *First of all*, it is the same day of the Lord from the morning star to the sunrise. The entire stretch is identical in essence and differs only in degree. If we are delivered from the day of the Lord, we are delivered from all of it. *Secondly*, the Lord's coming for the church is represented in prophetic typology by the morning star. We will be raptured when the morning star appears, well before the dawning of the day. This is a pretribulation rapture.

The following chart illustrates the four aspects of the day of the Lord. The rapture is the morning star. The tribulation is the dawning of the day. The second coming is the sunrise of the day. The millennium is the day proper.

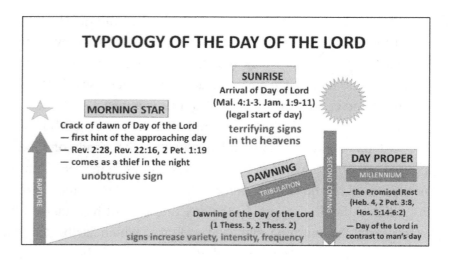

Revelation 3:10

My favorite argument for a pretribulation rapture is the promise in Revelation 3:10, which I provide below in both a literal translation and a paraphrase.

> Because you have kept the matter of my patience, I also will keep you from the hour of trial, which shall come upon all the world, to try them that dwell upon Earth. — *literal*

Because you have patiently suffered with me in the church age, I will remove you from the planet before the tribulation, which shall come upon the entire planet, to try those whose focus is only earthly. — *paraphrase*

This verse contains six distinct nuggets of revelation that point us in the direction of the correct understanding of this verse: the extent of the trial, the focus of the trial, exemption from the trial, the matter of Christ's patience, the manner of exemption, and the meaning of trial.

1—The extent of the trial. The hour of trial comes upon ALL the world. This is critical. This is quantitatively distinct from the entire gamut of trials that the world faced in the church age. No visitation since the flood has engulfed the entire planet. The flood destroyed the world that then was and resurfaced the entire planet. So it will be at the end of the age. The visitations of the hour of trial, which climax with the great day of God Almighty, will turn the world to rubble and ash. Now IF the hour of trial comes upon the entire planet, THEN there will be no way for mankind to escape that awful hour except for supernatural removal from the hour. This implies that the Lord must and will remove the church from the planet before this hour starts.

2—*The focus of the trial.* This trial falls upon those that "dwell upon Earth," in other words "the earth-dwellers." This is a theological term that refers to those humans whose hearts and lives are wrapped up in Earth and its concerns, in contrast to those who are pilgrims and strangers on it.[3] It refers to the exact same group of unsaved humans as terms like the unbelievers, the unrighteous, and the ungodly, but it focuses on their earthiness. Their lives are completely wrapped up in what the world has to offer. They have no interest in matters eternal or divine. The hour of trial, then, is intended to try the earth-dwellers, not the body

45

of Christ. Any theory that claims that this hour of trial pertains to the church has tossed the plain statement of the verse in the dumpster.

3—Exemption from the trial. The first half of the verse states, "Because you have kept the matter of my patience, I also will keep you from the hour of trial." Notice the words "keep you from." This is an exemption from the hour of trial that shall come upon the entire world. Who gets this exemption? Those who have kept the matter of the Lord's patience. This needs clarification. This is not a reward for exceptional performance. There is no hint here of a partial rapture. This is a statement of faith viewed through the lens of the patience of faith. All who believe will enjoy this promise, no matter how weak or broken.

4—The matter of his patience. What does it mean to keep the matter of the Lord's patience? It simply means that believers can't be persuaded to turn away from following Jesus by a world that hates the Jesus of the Bible and the Bible of Jesus. This is not a statement of exceptional attainment as a disciple. It is a simple statement of faith, faith that sees the believer kept by the power of God through thick and thin. Our weak faith taps into the infinite resources of the infinite God, who strengthens us in the inner man. We can do and endure all things through Christ.

The church, whose citizenship is in heaven, lives in a world whose god and ruler is Satan. This foul being, manifesting his headship through the unseen realm, has turned the world into a sewer of unbelief and iniquity. This means that believers find themselves in an endless string of situations that demand faith and patience on their part. "In patience possess your souls" (Luke 21:19). Throughout this age it has been, and is, the believer's lot to share in the fellowship of Christ's sufferings (Phil. 3:10) and Christ's patience (Rev 3:10). But the time of trials will come to an end. Some sweet day soon, the rapture trumpet will sound, and all who have kept the matter of Christ's patience—that is, all who are believers—will meet the Lord in the clouds and thus be kept from the hour of trial that is coming upon the world.

5—The manner of exemption. The verse plainly states that the Lord will *keep* his church *from* the hour of trial. Note the words KEEP FROM. This phrase does not mean *keep from harm* while in the hour or *preserve* while in the hour or *protect* while in the hour. It means *keep from the hour*, which implies removal prior to the hour.

Think about how we use this phrase in English. *Keep from* a train wreck does not mean *preserve in* a train wreck. *Keep from* hell does not mean *protect in* hell. *Keep from* a trial does not mean *keep safe in* the trial. In all of these instances, the delivered are kept away from the situation, not protected in the situation. Assigning the sense of *protect through* to the words *keep from* is contrary to English use and often leads to nonsense. So it is with *keep from* the hour in Revelation 3:10. If we allow these words to have their usual English sense, the phrase can only mean that the church will not enter the hour. She will be removed from Earth before the hour begins.

An appeal to the Greek gains nothing for those who want to force this verse to testify that the church will go through the tribulation. The use of τηρέω ἐκ (tēreō ek) follows the same path as *keep from* in English. Moreover, the Greeks had a verb to express *keep through*, which was διατηρέω (diatēreō). For those who want to see examples of how these two verbs were used in Greek, refer to the endnotes.[4]

The conclusion is certain if we let the passage speak for itself. IF the hour comes upon the whole world, and IF the church is kept from the hour, THEN the church must be removed from

Earth before the hour begins. This is a pretribulation rapture. The coming King will remove his church from the planet before he brings sweeping judgment upon the planet.

Now some try to overthrow the above understanding with the observation that *keep from* (tēreō ek) is also used in John 17, "I don't pray that you would take them out of the world, but that you would *keep* them *from* the evil one." They pose a challenge that stumbles many: if *keep from* doesn't take the church out of the world in John 17, why would anyone think that it takes the church out of the world in Revelation 3:10? But this argument is comparing apples to oranges. The two passages actually present two very different *keep-from* scenarios.

The *keep-from* scenario in John 17 concerns spiritual warfare during the church age. The church age is the time of Christ's patience, when his followers are granted the honor of following the rejected, crucified Messiah in this God-hating, devil-filled world. During this time, the Lord does not remove his followers from the battlefield (from Earth). Rather, he protects them by *keeping* them *from* the evil one on the battlefield.

What does "*keep from* the evil one" mean? It means that God puts spiritual distance between us and Satan. Not distance in the sense of feet, but distance in the sense of spiritual protection. He protects us from being ruined or destroyed by the enemy. He has placed limits on what the enemy can do to us, even as he placed limits on what he could do to Job. The adversary can discourage believers, but he can't break them. He can stumble believers and knock them down, but he can't keep them down. He can defile them in a superficial way. He can't defile them in a substantial way. He can't steal their grace, their faith, their hope, or their salvation. Though the outward man perishes, the inward man is renewed day by day (2 Cor. 4:16).

The same message is taught in 1 John 5:18 but with the addition of God's method of preservation. "He that is born of God keeps himself, and the wicked one doesn't touch him." This is not a statement of self-sufficiency or self-sanctification. It is a statement of divine provision. Those who have been born again have been regenerated and energized in their heart by the power of the Holy Spirit, and this power provides the believer with the ability to withstand all the wiles and attacks of the enemy and still be standing when the dust settles. We can lose some battles, but we can't lose the war.

The *keep-from* scenario in Revelation 3:10 concerns the hour of trial (the tribulation) that follows the church age. Those who kept the matter of Christ's patience during the church age—indeed, were kept from the evil one on the battlefield—will be *kept from* the hour of trial which falls upon the entire world.

6—The meaning of trial. Some claim that the Greek word translated *trial* here, πειρασμός (*peirasmos*), is never used for judgment or wrath. On this basis of this claim, they insist that Revelation 3:10 can't be talking about judgment upon the world, but must be talking about the believers undergoing a great trial of persecution under the antichrist.

This is one of those common sound bites that sway the multitudes but have no foundation in reality. This word is used in the Bible and Koine literature for judgment and wrath, even in extinction-level degrees. In 2 Peter 2:9, for instance, we find it used in reference to the fiery judgment that fell on Sodom.

The Lord knows how to deliver the godly from a TRIAL and reserve the unjust for punishment in the day of JUDGMENT.

Two things stand out here. First of all, *trial* is used in parallel with the day of judgment.[5] This tells us that *trial* can be used as a synonym for *judgment*. Secondly, the judgment here was the fire that fell from heaven and destroyed Sodom and Gomorrha, leaving not a trace of those once glorious cities. This tells us that *peirasmos* can be used for extinction-level judgments. Indeed, the trial that fell upon Sodom in Lot's day is used in the Bible as a type of the fiery judgment that shall fall on the world in the last days and incinerate the entire planet.

We also find the word *peirasmos* used in the Septuagint in Deuteronomy 4:34 in reference to the judgments that fell on Egypt at the time of Israel's exodus.

> Or has God ever tried to go and take for himself a nation from the midst of another nation by TRIALS, signs, wonders, war, a mighty hand and an outstretched arm, and by terrifying deeds, like all the things that the Lord your God did for you in Egypt before your eyes?

These two examples should settle the question for any honest student. The Greek word *peirasmos* was used for a wide range of things: from simple tests (as for genuineness or hardness) to devastating judgments and manifestations of wrath that don't fall under the pale of *trial* in English.

The bottom line. When we investigate the six nuggets of information in this verse, we come to the conclusion that the hour of trial falls upon the entire planet, that its focus is the ungodly (the earth-dwellers), that the word *trial* is expansive enough to include everything from the trial of the antichrist to the severest judgments in the day of the Lord, that believers will be exempt from the hour of trial, that their exemption is based on trusting Christ in the time of his patience (the church age), and that this exemption removes the church from the hour of trial, which boils down to removal from Earth. These six points absolutely demand a pretribulation rapture.

John 14:1-3

One of my favorite arguments for a pretribulation rapture is found in John 14:1-3. On the eve of his crucifixion, the Lord informed his disciples that he was departing to his Father's house, that he would prepare a place for them there, and that he would return for them.

> In my Father's house are many mansions. If it were not so, I would have told you. I go to prepare a place for you. And if I go and prepare a place for you, I will come again and receive you to myself; that where I am, there you may be also.

Where did Jesus go when he left Earth? Heaven! Where is he now? In heaven! Where is the place that he is preparing for us? In heaven! Where will we be going when the Lord comes again for his church? Heaven! This should thrill us. When Jesus comes for us, he will take us to the heavenly city, where we will find eternal residence in the Father's house in quarters custom-built for us by the Master Carpenter himself.

Now some try to empty this passage of its rapture promise by claiming that the Father's house refers to the temple of God in Jerusalem. But this is a stretch. The Lord Jesus didn't go to the temple in Jerusalem at his ascension. He went to heaven. He isn't building us mansions in the earthly temple. He can't be. The temple was destroyed in AD 70. No, the house in question can only be the Father's eternal house in New Jerusalem, a house which will stay separate from Earth until the thousand years are completed. Then the heavenly city will descend from heaven, and God will dwell among mankind forever. He will be our Father, and we shall be his children. At that time, for all practical purposes, heaven will have moved to Earth.

Now the journey to heaven to live with Christ in the Father's house implies a pretribulation rapture. How so? First of all, the salient facts prove that it can't be the second coming. At the second coming the saints on Earth are gathered sideways to Israel for the sheep and goats judgment, and then they stay down here. They don't travel to heaven. At the second coming the saints in heaven descend for the battle of Armageddon (Rev. 19, Joel 2, Is. 13), and then they stay down here to reign with Christ in his kingdom. But when Christ comes for his church, the saints travel to heaven and stay there.

Secondly, the salient facts imply a significant amount of time between the journey to heaven and the journey back down at the second coming. Observe that our Lord has now invested *nearly two thousand years in construction* preparing mansions for his church. This does not harmonize with a u-turn trip to heaven, or even a few-months visit. You don't put that kind of effort into projects that will only see temporary use. The tremendous effort implies habitation, not vacation or momentary examination. Consider the *reception*, where the Lord receives the saints into the family of God and the *stay*—"Where I am, there you may be." Together they imply a span of time sufficient to learn the ropes for the duties, formalities, and privileges of the believers. This is when the saints learn their roles as bride, as coregents, as children and heirs of God, as coheirs with Christ. This isn't learned by osmosis. It can't be learned in a day.

When we actually let John 14:1-3 say and mean what it wants to say and mean, then it becomes obvious that the journey to heaven in this passage implies a significant stay that corresponds with a pretribulation rapture.

2 Thessalonians 2:1-3

Many folks point to 2 Thessalonians 2:1-3 as proof that the rapture will not happen until after the tribulation. They believe that the first two verses equate the rapture and the day of the Lord, and that verse three states that the rapture won't happen until after the antichrist has been revealed. This understanding is based on modern translations like the ESV below.

> (1) Now CONCERNING the coming of our Lord Jesus Christ and our being gathered together to him, we ask you, brothers, (2) not to be quickly shaken in mind or alarmed, either by a spirit or a spoken word, or a letter seeming to be from us, to the effect that the day of the Lord HAS COME. (3) Let no one deceive you in any way. For that day WILL NOT COME, unless the rebellion comes first, and the man of lawlessness is revealed.

Notice the translation *concerning*. This implies to many that the coming of the day of the Lord in verse two is commentary on the coming of the Lord and the gathering of the church in verse one. In other words, the instruction on the day of the Lord is instruction on the circumstances and timing of the rapture.

Notice further that "*that day will not come*" in verse three refers back to the day of the Lord in verse two. This implies, to those who equate the church's gathering in verse one with the day of the Lord in verse two, that the rapture can't come until after the antichrist has been revealed.

But this is a misunderstanding of this passage. It does not equate the rapture and the day of the Lord. It contrasts them. The timing and circumstances of the day of the Lord in verses two and three are not to be construed as the timing and circumstances of the rapture. Rather, the timing and circumstances of the day of the Lord are given in contradistinction to the rapture.

Indeed, it was this very passage, being read in the Greek, that convinced J.N. Darby of the pretribulation rapture.[6] I would add that studying this passage in the Greek played a pivotal role in my understanding too, confirming me in the truth of a rapture before the tribulation.

So how does this passage contrast the rapture and the day of the Lord? Fundamental grammar. Two considerations must be addressed. The first is the translation of ἐνέστηκεν (enestēken),[7] translated *has come* in verse two and *will not come* with the negation in verse three. The second consideration is the full petition format which, when recognized, sheds much light on the right understanding of the passage.

I here provide my emendation of the King James version because it handles the translation of ἐνέστηκεν (enestēken) and the translation of the full petition better than the popular modern translations.

> (1) Now we BESEECH you, brethren, BY the coming of our Lord Jesus Christ and our gathering together unto him, (2) THAT YOU BE NOT SOON SHAKEN in mind, or be troubled, neither by spirit, nor by word, nor by letter as from us, as that the day of the Lord IS PRESENT. (3) Let no man deceive you by any means: for that day IS NOT PRESENT, except there come a falling away first, and the man of sin be revealed, the son of perdition.

The first thing to point out is that I have translated the verb ἐνέστηκεν (enestēken) by *is present* and by *is not present* when negated. This is the best translation. But *has come* and *has not come* are workable. They present the same *present* force, just not as forcefully. Sadly, most versions blunder on the negation, introducing the future tense. The KJV renders it *shall not come*, the NKJV, NASB, and ESV offer *will not come*. This gives the wrong sense. It implies that the revelation of the antichrist is a condition for the dawning of the day of the Lord. But Paul's argument states something radically different. It states that the antichrist is the proof that the day of the Lord is here. If you see the antichrist, you know that you are in the day of the Lord.

The second thing to point out is that the passage is a standard petition in its full form—that is, it employs all three potential parts of a petition: the verb of petition, the petition itself, and the ὑπέρ (huper) clause that provides the reason or purpose for the petition. Anyone who has actually spent time reading Koine or Classical Greek literature will recognize the pattern, in both its partial and full formats.

Since this is a commonplace petition, the structure here should be handled the same way that scholars handle it in extra-biblical literature. Sadly, this frequently is not the case. Modern translations and commentaries often treat this passage as if it featured rare or non-standard Greek.[8] It is my suspicion that this is traced to prejudice against the pretribulation rapture.

Let's examine the three parts of the petition—the verb, the petition, and the ὑπέρ (huper) clause. If we let them have the same force here that they have everywhere else in Greek literature, then they will tell a very different story than the post-tribulation interpretation that many are familiar with.

The petition verb. The verb is ἐρωτάω (erōtaō), which means *request, beseech, intreat*. It is translated *beseech* in the KJV, *ask* in the NKJV and ESV, and *request* in the NASB. This, indisputably, is a verb of petition. That should inform everyone that the passage is a petition, that the passage should be handled as a petition, and that interpreters should be looking for the grammatical parts of a petition. Nonetheless, many treat the passage as if it were an explanation that tells the believers *about* the rapture rather than a petition that beseeches the believers *by* or *on account of* the rapture. This is a significant difference in hermeneutical approach, one that misdirects the interpretation.

The request. The request that Paul made was that the Thessalonians "be not soon shaken ... as if the day of the Lord were present." We could paraphrase this as, "Don't be worried that you might be in the day of the Lord." Why did Paul make this request? Severe persecution combined with bad teaching had led the Thessalonians to fear that they were in the day of the Lord—the time of great tribulation. Paul was attempting to allay this fear.

The request was followed with a clarification on the day of the Lord. "Don't let anyone deceive you by any means, for that day is not present unless the falling away has first come and the man of sin has been revealed." His point is unmistakable. The antichrist is the chief proof that the world has entered the time of the dawning of the day of the Lord. If you see the antichrist, you are in the day of the Lord. If you don't see the antichrist, then you are not in the day of the Lord.

One further thought here. The antichrist and the apostasy are inseparable. They are two sides same coin. The apostasy is initiated when Israel accepts a covenant with the antichrist at the start of the seventieth week. It reaches its climax when Israel worships the antichrist at the midpoint of the week.

The ὑπὲρ (huper) clause. In petitions in Greek, the ὑπὲρ (huper) clause gives the reason or ground of the petition. The petition was "Don't worry that you might be in the day of the Lord." The reason for the petition is "*by* the coming of the Lord and our gathering together unto him." This boils down to "*on account of* the rapture." What does this mean? To the English ear, it seems a bit fuzzy. The fuzziness clears up if we render it "*because of* the rapture." Paul is telling the Thessalonians, "You don't need to worry about finding yourselves in the day of the Lord because we are going up in the rapture."

Potent Argument. If we embrace all three parts of the petition in 2 Thessalonians 2:1-3—and we will if we apply the historical-grammatical hermeneutic with any reasonable degree of knowledge and consistency—then we will conclude that Paul is presenting the pretribulation rapture as the reason not to worry about the day of the Lord.

His potent argument, which resembles a prosecuting attorney tearing apart an allegation, can be summarized as follows. "We plead with you not to worry about the reports that we might be in the dawning of the day of the Lord [the tribulation]. There are two reasons that we can't be in that time. The first is that we are going up in the rapture, not through the day of the Lord." The second is that the antichrist is the proof that the day of the Lord has dawned. Look around. If you don't see the antichrist publicly revealed down here on Earth, then we are not in the day of the Lord. The tribulation has not yet started.

CHART OF THE PETITION IN 2 THESS. 2:1-3

	Greek	Meaning	KJV (modified)
Verb of request	ἐρωτῶμεν δὲ ὑμᾶς	We ask you	We beseech you
The request	εἰς τὸ μὴ ταχέως σαλευθῆναι ὑμᾶς … ὡς ὅτι ἐνέστηκεν ἡ ἡμέρα τοῦ Κυρίου	Don't fear that you are in the day of the Lord	That you be not soon shaken … as that the day of the Lord is present.
Reason for request	ὑπὲρ τῆς παρουσίας τοῦ κυρίου ἡμῶν Ἰησοῦ Χριστοῦ καὶ ἡμῶν ἐπισυναγωγῆς ἐπ' αὐτόν	Because of our Lord's coming … and our rapture unto him	By the coming of our Lord … and our gathering together unto him
Second reason	ὅτι [οὐ ἐνέστηκεν ἡ ἡμέρα τοῦ Κυρίου] ἐὰν μὴ ἔλθῃ ἡ ἀποστασία πρῶτον καὶ ἀποκαλυφθῇ ὁ ἄνθρωπος τῆς ἁμαρτίας	because the day of the Lord isn't here if you don't see the antichrist	for that day is not present, except there come a falling away first, and the man of sin be revealed,

The Seventieth Week is the Wrath of God

The arguments that were presented in this chapter make a strong case that wrath and tribulation are used interchangeably, that both terms are used to refer to the seventieth week, and that the promise of deliverance from the wrath to come will see the church removed from Earth before the seventieth week. This is a pretribulation rapture.

A few corroborating arguments were also presented. It was observed that the time of the antichrist is labeled the day of the Lord (2 Thess. 2:1-3) and that the antichrist is a judgment from God (2 Thess. 2:8-12). This means that the entire seventieth week is the wrath of God. And if the seventieth week is the wrath of God, then the rapture must occur prior to the seventieth week. Again, this is a pretribulation rapture.

It was further observed that the church will be kept from the hour of trial which will come upon the entire planet (Rev. 3:10) and that the word *trial* was used in Greek for a wide spectrum of trials, from simple tests to extinction-level visitations like the fire that destroyed Sodom. This means that the hour of trial can include everything from the test of the antichrist (the first seal) to the world-consuming fire at the second coming. It also means, since the church is kept from the hour, that the church must be removed from the planet before the first seal is opened and the antichrist appears on the scene. This is a pretribulation rapture.

PROOF 5

THE CHURCH IN HEAVEN BEFORE THE TRIBULATION

The Twenty-Four Elders

In Revelation, in the fourth and fifth chapters, we observe twenty-four elders who are seated around the throne of God and worship him. Who are these beings? Many regard their identity as mysterious, even unknowable. But their identification is only mysterious for two reasons. First of all, men start with a sloppy allegorical hermeneutic rather than a robust literal hermeneutic. Secondly, men do not make full use of their God-given reason to analyze the available data in the God-given revelation. When we take the scriptures literally, and we use our God-given reason on the hints that the scriptures offer us, we quickly gain a clear and certain understanding of who the twenty-four elders are.

Five Bits of Limiting Data

In the fourth and fifth chapters of Revelation, we are given five bits of information that limit the identification of the twenty-four elders.

1—They are blood redeemed. "You have redeemed us to God by your blood" (Rev. 5:9).

2—They are seated on thrones. "Round about the throne were twenty-four thrones, and upon the thrones I saw twenty-four elders sitting" (Rev. 4:4). They are not seated on chairs (as the KJV says) but on thrones.

3—They are wearing reward crowns. "They had on their heads crowns of gold" (Rev. 4:4). They are not wearing the royal crown (diadēma) but the reward crown (stephanos).

4—They have their resurrection robes. "Clothed in white robes" (Rev. 4:4). This is the literal robe that all the believers receive in the resurrection, which symbolizes their justification.

5—They possess all the aforementioned blessings in heaven before the tribulation starts. This is clear from the fact that they are seen in the throne room of God, seated on thrones, wearing their robes and crowns, before the first seal is opened and the antichrist revealed (Rev. 6:1).

The Data Restricts The Identity of the Elders

When we take the above bits of information and apply them to the options for the identity of the twenty-four elders, we are forced to exclude the following options.

1—They can't be angels. The elders have been bought by the blood of Christ. This is a huge clue. Redemption doesn't cover angels. It only covers humans. Christ took upon himself human nature, not angelic nature (Phil. 2:7, Heb. 2:16). He died for mankind alone. Thus, the elders must be human beings.

2—They can't be Old Testament saints or tribulation martyrs. The elders are in heaven *before* the tribulation, seated on thrones, wearing their robes and crowns. They are already rewarded. This means that they have already participated in the resurrection. This forbids identifying them as Old Testament saints or tribulation martyrs. Those two classes don't receive their rewards until they are raised at the second coming.

3—They are not New Testament saints patiently waiting for the resurrection. The elders are seated on thrones in the throne room of God, wearing their white robes and crowns. This means that they can't be New Testament saints waiting for the resurrection. If they have their rewards already, then they have already experienced the resurrection.

Once we have eliminated these three possibilities, there is only one left. The twenty-four elders can only be the representatives of the church who were glorified in the rapture, rewarded shortly thereafter, and are now in the throne room of God waiting for the Lord to open the first seal and begin his kingdom work.

Come Up Here!

Once we grasp the identification of the twenty-four elders, we are in a place to appreciate the type in Revelation 4:1.

> After these things I looked, and behold, a door stood open in heaven. And the first voice which I heard was like a trumpet speaking with me, saying, COME UP HERE, and I will show you things which must take place after this.

This journey to heaven is a type of the pretribulation rapture. It follows the church age in the second and third chapters, presents the church in the throne room of God in the fourth and fifth chapters, and precedes the start of the tribulation with the opening of the seals in the sixth chapter. Revelation 4:1 is the last time the church is seen on Earth in the book of Revelation until her descent with the Lord at Armageddon in chapter 19. She goes up at the rapture prior to the tribulation and descends again with the Lord after the tribulation.

The Twenty-four Courses

So who are the twenty-four elders? Some suggest that they are the twelve apostles and twelve patriarchs. I think this is unlikely. The twelve apostles are assigned to reign with Christ over the twelve tribes of Israel (Matt. 19:28). The twelve patriarchs will likely have similar responsibilities. The twenty-four elders, on the contrary, are assigned to work in the throne room of the Father, which is in New Jerusalem.

We need to go to the Old Testament to find the necessary clue for the identity of the elders. The biblical precedence for twenty-four men worshipping God in his throne room is found in the account of King David establishing twenty-four courses of priests for the temple service, in obedience to the command that the Lord had given Aaron (1 Chron. 24:1-19). As there were twenty-four courses of priests for the temple service in the Old Testament, so there must be twenty-four courses of priests in the New Testament priesthood. This is not the New Testament copying the pattern seen in the Old Testament. It is actually the other way around. The arrangement and order of the temple in the Old Testament was patterned after the arrangement and order of the true temple in heaven (Heb. 8:5).

> Which serve as an example and shadow of heavenly things, as Moses was admonished of God when he was about to make the tabernacle: See to it, he said, that you make all things according to the pattern shown you on the mount.

The twenty-four elders, therefore, are likely the heads of the twenty-four courses of the heavenly, New Testament priesthood. The courses will maintain a continuous presence in the throne room of God for all eternity. Each course will serve two weeks of the year in temple service. Four times per year all of the courses will be present. Whether the head of each course is a permanent post or a rotating post is uncertain.

A Potent Pretrib Argument

The twenty-four elders, once identified, provide us with perhaps the most potent argument for a pretribulation rapture in the Bible. They can't be angels because they are redeemed by the blood of the Lamb. They can't be Old Testament saints waiting for their resurrection at the second coming because they already have their rewards. They can't be New Testament saints waiting for their resurrection because they already have their rewards. They can only be New Testament saints who have already enjoyed the resurrection.

The timeline of the twenty-four elders absolutely demands a pretribulation rapture. The sequence starts with a summons to heaven which is a type of the rapture summons—"Come up here!" (Rev. 4:1). The twenty-four appear in the throne room, resurrected and rewarded (Rev. 4-5), prior to the opening of the first seal, which releases the antichrist (Rev. 6:1-2). This means that they shall not see the antichrist, or the seventieth week, or the tribulation. This is a pretribulation rapture.

PROOF 6

TYPES OF THE RAPTURE

The Proper Use of Typology

We don't get our doctrine from typology. That is a path to doctrinal disaster. Sound doctrine comes first. We recognize a picture of the truth (for that is what a type is) only after we have become familiar with the truth. But once we are grounded in the truth, the types for that truth will present themselves in the pages of scripture, and those types will be corroborating proof that we are on the right path.

Now the typologies in the Bible are numerous, but they are not all of the same caliber. They range from vague sketches to clear portrayals. The stronger our grasp on biblical doctrine, the stronger our grasp on biblical typology. Thankfully, the core doctrines of the Bible come with clear typologies that are easily recognized by all serious students of the word of God. When people point them out, they see them readily. When they find them on their own, the resemblance is undeniable.

I first experienced this as a babe in the Lord while reading the Old Testament through for the first time after having read the New Testament several times. When I came to Genesis 22 and read the account of Abraham offering his son Isaac, I was stunned. My jaw almost fell off my face. God stopped him and provided his own sacrifice. Despite the fact that I had never heard about biblical typology, I immediately knew that this was a picture of God offering his own Son. Since that glorious hour, typology has become a source of great blessing for me in both the illumination of truth and the confirmation of the inspiration of scripture. It is one of the greatest treasures in the Bible.

Four Favorite Types of the Rapture

There are numerous types of the pretribulation rapture in the Bible. In this chapter I will only cover four—my favorites. Three are powerful rapture types that are often overlooked: Abraham looking down on the plains of Sodom from Mamre, the ship suddenly being at land when the Lord came to his disciples in the storm, and the mysterious absence of Daniel when the three Hebrew lads were thrown in the furnace. The fourth is one that often faces strong objection from opponents of the pretribulation rapture: Enoch's journey to heaven before the flood.

In my handling of Enoch, I present a defense of using him as a type of the rapture. This will be an encouragement to those who are stumbled by the fierce opposition to this type and feel like they don't have an adequate response. The other three types should broaden the horizon of rapture typology for many, which will help forward the truth of the pretribulation rapture.

Obviously, there are typologies that I haven't included in this chapter. They were left out for two reasons. Some because they are well known and don't require special apologetic attention. Some because they aren't clear enough to me. I don't want to draw attention to less clear types that remind me of modern art, where seeing Bible truth appears to lie more in the imagination of the observer than in the intent of the painter.

The Translation of Enoch

Scripture records Enoch being taken up to heaven prior to the flood. We read in Genesis 5:24, "Enoch walked with God and was not, for God took him." This event is also referenced in Hebrews 11:5 with further information supplied.

> By faith Enoch was translated so that he should not see death; and was not found, because God had translated him: for before his translation he had this testimony, that he pleased God.

Enoch's translation to heaven before the flood is a type of the church being raptured before the time of God's judgment upon Earth, popularly called the tribulation.

Now some people reject Enoch's translation as a type of the pretribulation rapture. They point out that the patriarch actually ascended to heaven hundreds of years before the flood. In their minds, this forbids him from being a type of the rapture a few months before the tribulation. However, this rejection is based on a misunderstanding of how typology works. The types in the Bible are founded on the Bible's presentation of the matter, not on the full history of the matter.

The Bible, for instance, presents Melchizedek the high priest in Genesis 14, when he met Abraham, without giving us his parental lineage. Paul commented on this in Hebrews 7:3:

> Without father, without mother, without genealogy, having neither beginning of days nor end of life, but made like the Son of God, remains a priest continually.

Does this imply that Melchizedek is the eternal Son of God himself? No. He can't be the preincarnate Jesus. Notice that he is "made like the Son of man." If he was Jesus, he wouldn't need to be made like Jesus. The fact that he is made like Jesus tells us that he is a mere man. This means that he had earthly parents and that he had a birth day and a death day. Therefore, we are forced to conclude that it is the Bible's presentation of Melchizedek that paints him as a type of the fatherless and motherless Messiah, not his actual lineage. The parents are irrelevant to the type. The type lies entirely in the Bible's presentation.

In the same way, the centuries between Enoch's translation and the flood are irrelevant. The type lies entirely in the Bible's presentation of the matter, not the full historical account of it. The Bible presents Enoch and the flood in close proximity, and it presents Enoch going up before the time of judgment. This is all that matters.

Abraham on the High Plains of Mamre

I love the type of the rapture that we see in the account of Abraham in Genesis 18-19. When judgment was about to fall on Sodom, Abraham was enjoying fellowship with Jehovah and the angels on the high plains of Mamre, overlooking the scene of impending catastrophe. They even shared a meal. This pictures the church enjoying fellowship in heaven with the Lord and the angels immediately prior to judgment falling on Earth below.

In the big picture, Abraham is a type of the heavenly saints observing the judgment from above while Lot is a type of the earthly saints being delivered from judgment by the skin of their teeth. Notice that both Lot and his wife fled the scene of judgment, yet his wife didn't finish the escape she started. She perished in the way when she looked back. This fits the fleeing saints in the tribulation, but it doesn't fit the experience of the raptured saints very well. Nobody will be taken to the clouds yet perish before they get to New Jerusalem.

Instantaneous Deliverance From the Storm

In John 6:15-21, we read an incredible story that presents an amazing, indeed a profound, type of the rapture.

> When Jesus therefore perceived that they would come and take him by force to make him a king, he departed again to a mountain by himself. When evening was come, his disciples went down unto the sea, and entered into a ship, and went over the sea toward Capernaum. And it became dark, and Jesus was not come to them. And the sea arose because a strong wind blew. So when they had rowed twenty-five or thirty furlongs, they saw Jesus walking on the sea and nearing the ship, and they were afraid. But he said to them, "It is I, don't be afraid." Then they received him into the ship, and immediately the ship was at the land where they were headed.

In the evening, his disciples set sail. This is a picture of the church setting sail across the sea of life. Spiritually speaking, it was evening when the church age began. About four thousand years (four figurative days) had passed since creation. About two thousand years (two figurative days) remained before God's sabbath rest (the millennium) arrived. So the church was two-thirds of the way through the figurative week when she began her journey. It was the evening of the age. The end was near.

Jesus departed again to a mountain by himself. When the disciples began their journey, the Lord had already departed to an overlooking mountaintop. This pictures the ascended Lord in heaven watching over his church as they undertake their pilgrim journey across the sea of life.

It became dark, and the sea arose because a strong wind blew. This pictures the church facing a violent storm at the end of the age, one that surpasses all that she had faced in the past. Even now the mystery of iniquity is brewing a storm of satanic agenda and deception in the world that is strengthening rapidly. The winds are already disturbing the sea of life and rocking our boat. This storm will continue to strengthen in preparation for the tribulation. We should not be surprised if we find ourselves experiencing discomfort and dread as we wait for the Lord.

Jesus was not come to them. When the storm first whips up, the disciples are still in their small boat on the sea, and Jesus is still on the mountaintop. This pictures the fact that when the storm of new world order iniquity breaks upon the world at the tail end of the church age, the Lord is still in heaven. While we will not see the brunt of the storm in the tribulation, we could see some rough sailing before the Lord comes and takes us out of this world.

They saw Jesus … they received him … and immediately the ship was at the land where they were headed. When the disciples saw Jesus, realized that it was him, and received him, they got a very pleasant surprise. In a moment, the ship was in safe harbor, the very harbor they were rowing for. Notice that in this instance, the storm isn't miraculously stopped. The ship is miraculously moved. The Lord came to his disciples shortly after the storm had arisen and rescued them. They were vouchsafed a small taste of the storm, and then were removed from it. They didn't have to go through it.

This event pictures the rapture. The Lord will come to his church while she is toiling away at the start of a ferocious storm of iniquity here on Earth. When she welcomes him, she will be immediately transported to her safe harbor, even the glorious city, New Jerusalem. We won't go through the storm. We will be delivered from it. But we could experience, indeed we already are experiencing, the leading edge of the storm as the global cabal rolls out its platform of new-world-order iniquity in their heinous preparation for the tribulation.

Daniel and the Hebrew Youths

When the three Hebrew young men—Shadrach, Meshach, and Abednego—are thrown into the fiery furnace in the third chapter of Daniel, Daniel is mysteriously missing. Where was he? If he had been present in the land, surely he would not have been exempt from the connivery and persecution. So we must assume that he was absent, perhaps in a distant land on a foreign mission.

Daniel's absence seems to me to be a picture of the rapture as it affects the Jews in the last days. One of the godly Jews is mysteriously absent in a situation where he would normally be expected to be found. The other godly Jews will be forced to endure the fires of tribulation, and they will be mysteriously preserved. What an amazing picture of the believing Jews in the last days. Some mysteriously removed. Others mysteriously protected. All mysteriously blessed.

This type implies that three times as many born again Jews will be preserved through the tribulation as will be preserved by the rapture before the tribulation. I wouldn't be surprised if this approximates the truth. I do believe that there will be an amazing revival among the Jews after the rapture.

Pictures of the Pretrib Rapture

In this chapter we examined four vivid typologies of a pretribulation rapture, all viewing this glorious event from different perspectives: Enoch's translation prior to the flood, Abraham fellowshipping on the high plains of Mamre with Jehovah and the angels while fire fell on Sodom, the disciples being miraculously and instantaneously delivered to safe harbor when a fierce storm broke upon them, and Daniel being mysteriously absent from the scene when his Jewish brethren were placed in a fiery trial. Such pictures of a pretribulation rapture would not be found in the God-inspired, God-given Bible unless it actually did teach a pretribulation rapture.

PROOF 7

THE COMING OF THE SON OF MAN

Matthew 24:36-44

Matthew 24:36-44 is one of the most overlooked and underappreciated passages on the rapture. This is tragic. This passage provides vital information on the circumstances and timing of the Lord's coming for the church.

> But no man knows that day and hour, no, not even the angels of heaven, but only my Father. But as the days of Noah were, so shall also the coming of the Son of man be. For as in the days before the flood men were eating and drinking, marrying and giving in marriage, until the day that Noah entered into the ark, and were oblivious [of impending judgment] until the flood came and took them all away; so also shall the coming of the Son of man be. Then two men shall be in the field: one shall be taken and the other left. Two women shall be grinding at the mill: one shall be taken and the other left. Watch therefore, for you do not know what hour your Lord is coming. But know this, that if the master of the house had known what hour the thief would come, he would have watched and would not have allowed his house to be broken into. Therefore be ready, for the Son of man is coming at an hour that you do not expect.

In this passage we find several distinct arguments that point to a pretribulation rapture: the days of Noah, the thief in the night, and relative normality.

The Days of Noah

In Matthew 24:36-44 we read the prediction, "As the days of Noah were, so also shall the coming of the Son of man be." This is a dire indictment of the world's character. In God's estimation, the moral climate of the world at the time of the coming of the Son of man—particularly in the fractured Roman empire and Israel—will reflect the moral climate that prevailed in the days before the flood. The world will be filled with the same perversion, iniquity, and idolatry that brought the deluge upon the world in Noah's day. It will be as dark as the world can get.

But the moral climate of the last days is not the only truth pictured by Noah's experience. It also portrays the deliverance of the saints before the fall of judgment. Notice that Noah entered the ark before the flood and that God sealed the door shut. Those inside were perfectly and divinely preserved from judgment! This pictures the secured deliverance of the believers prior to the start of the last-days judgment.

Now there is debate as to whether this type is intended to picture the deliverance of the church prior to the tribulation or the deliverance of a remnant through the tribulation. This debate misses the obvious truth. Noah's deliverance fits both. It fits the church being removed from Earth before the tribulation, and it fits a Jewish remnant, sealed and set apart before the tribulation, being preserved through the tribulation.

Consider the temporal proximity and moral affinity of the two deliverances. The rapture of the church and the sealing of a

Jewish remnant occur only weeks or months apart. This means that the two deliverance scenarios have approximately the same relationship with the end of the age. They happen at nearly the same temperature in the moral climate of the last days. They transpire at nearly the same degree of stage setting for the tribulation. They occur at nearly the same distance from the opening of the first seal and the rise of the antichrist. This proximity and affinity is also illustrated by end-times typology: the rapture is pictured as the morning star (Rev. 2:28, Rev. 22:16, 2 Pet. 1:19) while the return to Israel is pictured as early dawn (Hos. 6:3, Ps. 46:5).

Bearing this spiritual symmetry in mind, it is reasonable to embrace Noah's deliverance as a type that was designed to suit the deliverance of both the church and Israel. I would remind the reader that Noah entered the ark prior to the onset of judgment, that God himself sealed the door of this vehicle of deliverance, and that the ark of salvation floated above the judgment. It is hard to miss that these aspects of Noah's experience picture a rapture prior to the tribulation.

The Thief in the Night

The coming of the Son of man in Matthew 24:36-44 is compared to a thief in the night. Thieves—think burglars—break in or sneak in during the night and steal things without anyone noticing. This implies that the coming of the Lord is going to steal upon the world and catch it by surprise, the same way that the start of the flood caught the world by surprise. This element of surprise indicates that this passage has the rapture aspect (the morning star aspect) of the coming of the Son of man in view, not the second coming aspect (the sunrise aspect).

At the second coming, when the Lord descends for the battle of Armageddon, the world will not be caught by surprise. The two witnesses will have warned the world for three and a half years. Their messages will spread around the globe on social media. The hundred and forty-four thousand will have fulfilled their ministry for the Lord, bearing a testimony of supernatural preservation and eternal truth. The remnant who have been empowered by the promise of the Spirit—promised in Joel 2 and partially fulfilled in the early chapters of Acts—will have shared the gospel in the power of the Spirit for most, if not all, of the seventieth week. The angels sent by God will have gone to the four corners of Earth, preaching the gospel, warning men to flee Babylon, and urging men not to take the mark of the beast (Rev. 14:6-10). Not a single soul will make it to the end of the tribulation without hearing the gospel preached accurately, powerfully, and supernaturally.

Moreover, the world will have experienced seven years of horrifying judgments that fulfilled the book of Revelation to the letter. This won't escape their attention. They will figure out, sooner or later, during the tribulation that God is the author of these visitations. For instance, after the fourth angel pours out his bowl, causing the sun to scorch mankind with intense heat, the world refuses to repent and give God glory. Instead, they blaspheme him (Rev. 16:8-9). For another example, after the fifth angel pours out his bowl, veiling the world in pitch-black darkness, the inhabitants of the world blaspheme the God of heaven (Rev. 16:10-11).

But the knowledge factor is upped even higher with the sixth bowl. When it is poured out, deceiving spirits go to the kings of the whole world and gather them with their armies to the valley of Megiddo for the battle that is popularly called Armageddon

(Rev. 16:14). This united effort of the world is also referred to in Psalm 2:1-4, where the kings of Earth take counsel against the Lord and his Anointed, desiring to rid themselves of their bonds and cords. There is zero surprise at this point in time. The world gathers at the right time and the right place to fight an invader they know is coming. Most likely, the governments of the world will paint the Lord's descent as an alien invasion.

Corroborating this lack of surprise at the second coming is the fact that this event is portrayed in scripture typology as the sunrise of the day of the Lord (Mal. 4:1-3). The rising of the sun doesn't take the world at large by surprise. By the time it climbs above the horizon, men are long forewarned and expecting it.

In stark contrast, the rapture before the tribulation will come as a total surprise. While the world is fast asleep, oblivious to the early warning signs and the warnings of the church, the Morning Star will come. In a moment, tens of millions of Christians will vanish around the world. Then the world will realize, with shock and alarm, that something extremely unusual—unprecedented—has happened that robbed the planet of tens of millions of people. They will search for answers, but they won't want to believe the real—the biblical—explanation for the vanishing. The thief has come in the night, and the day of the Lord is now dawning.

Relative Normality

Matthew 24:36-44 presents the world in a state of relative normality at the time of the coming of the Son of man. This is evident in the statement, "Men were eating and drinking, marrying and giving in marriage, until the day that Noah entered into the ark" (v. 38). Right up until the coming of the Son of man, the wheels of the world system are still turning normally. The troubles that mankind faces—as wars, disasters, upheavals—are well within the normal range of their troubles over the past few centuries. Nothing hints at troubles outside this range—except for the despised warnings of despised Christians. This gives the world a false sense of security. They go about their worldly business oblivious to the apocalyptic troubles on the horizon.

This complacency and obliviousness are at odds with the time of the second coming, the sunrise of the coming of the Son of man. At that time, the world will not be indulging a false sense of security. They will be wearied with years of apocalyptic-level visitations, and they will be busy intentionally gathering every army on the planet to Armageddon to fight the invader that they do not want to rule over them—the author of the visitations.

This complacency and obliviousness, on the other hand, are completely consistent with the time of the rapture prior to the tribulation, which is the morning star of the coming of the Son of man. While the world indulges relative normality and a false sense of security, not yet plagued by any of the visitations of the tribulation, it will be rattled by the sudden disappearance of tens of millions around the globe—the first extraordinary event of the last days. Millions will be shaken out of spiritual complacency by this event. Around the world, governments will scramble to calm the hysteria and explain the vanishings. Fairy tales like aliens, blue beams, and karma will all get some traction.

After the rapture, things will get very ugly very fast as God rolls out his campaign of shock and awe. In short order, the world will experience the war of Gog and Magog (Ez. 38-39), the rise of the antichrist, worldwide war and famine, colossal asteroids falling from the sky, supernatural manifestations like the demon-locust from hell, signs in the heavens, and finally Armageddon itself. The world will quickly progress from relative normality to off-the-charts abnormality.

IF we rightly apprehend the relative normality at the time of the coming of the Son of man that we see in Matthew 24:36-44, and IF we understand how insanely abnormal things will be in the tribulation, not to mention at the second coming, THEN we are forced to conclude that this passage is not addressing the sunrise of the coming of the Son of man (the second coming), but the morning star of the coming of the Son of man (the rapture). Relative normality, then, has the thief robbing the world prior to the tribulation. This is a pretribulation rapture.

Three-Strand Argument for Pretrib Rapture

In this chapter, we examined three identifying points on the coming of the Son of man in Matthew 24:36-44. The first is that the promised deliverance of the believers will come before the fall of judgment as it did in the days of Noah. The second is that the Lord will come like a thief in the night when he comes to deliver his saints. The third is that the world will be in a state of relative normality when the Lord comes for his saints. These points don't square with the second coming. The second coming doesn't happen before the judgment falls, nor does it come like a thief in the night, nor does it find the world in a state of relative normality. But these points do fit the rapture of the church. At that time, the Lord will deliver his saints before the fall of judgment, this deliverance will come upon the world like a thief in the night, and the world will be enjoying relative normality. Together these points make a three-strand argument for a pretribulation rapture. A three-strand cord is not quickly broken.

PROOF 8

THE NATURE OF THE SEALS

When Does the Wrath Begin?

The Bible is very clear that at the end of this age, God will pour out his wrath upon the world. Nobody who attempts to take prophecy literally disputes this. There is a dispute, however, on when this wrath begins. Does it include the entire seventieth week? Or only the latter part of it? Does it include the seals? Or are the seals excluded?

Pretribulationists believe that all of the visitations of the seventieth week, including the seals, are judgment. They believe that the day of the Lord begins with the rapture of the church, that glorious meeting in the clouds being the morning star of the day of the Lord.

The prewrath rapture advocates, on the contrary, insist that the seals are not judgment. In their estimation, the wars, famine, pestilence, and persecution introduced by the seals are merely more of the same man-caused problems that have roiled the world throughout the age. They insist that the sixth seal heralds the arrival of judgment and that the seven trumpets are the initial stage of judgment.

So who is correct? Are the seals judgment? I answer with a resounding, yes! This point is not difficult to establish if we let the testimony of scripture have a fair hearing. The following points highlight several strong reasons why the seals must be recognized as the initial expression of the wrath of God.

Qualitative Difference

The seals are qualitatively different than the normal course of problems that have plagued the world since the beginning of the church age. Only the Lamb is worthy to open the seals (Rev. 5:1-4). No one else in heaven, or on Earth, or under the earth is worthy to open them and introduce their contents. No man or angel is fit for this undertaking. No created being is worthy of this high calling. Only the Lord Jesus himself, the eternal Son of God, is worthy to receive them from the Father, open them, and unleash their contents, a veritable river of woes for the world.

The normal course of troubles that mankind faces does not require this direct involvement of the Lord. They are introduced by fallen men and angels acting on their own accord and by nature manifesting the normal effects of the curse. Neither fallen men, nor fallen angels, nor fallen nature require a special governmental act of the Lord to engage in their current activities. His only involvement with them is *providential*, restraining their efforts and limiting the damage that they can do. Moreover, these fallen actors don't have to meet any worthiness standard to bring pain and sorrow upon mankind in the normal course of troubles. Fallenness is the only criteria.

When the Lord takes the scroll in hand, his role in the government of the world officially changes. He is setting aside his *providential* government over this planet and taking up his *theocratic* government. His first act in this office is opening the seals. No longer is God restricting damage so man's troubles stay within the usual range. Now he unleashes the fallen realm and nature, allowing them to go on a rampage for the ages, one fully in keeping with his purposes for eschatological judgment and theocratic government.

Two aspects of the transition from providential government to theocratic government deserve further attention: the *result* when God ceases to restrain iniquity and the *aim* of God's theocratic (kingdom) work during the tribulation.

What will happen when God ceases to restrain the mystery of iniquity? The mystery of iniquity that God has been restraining will explode upon the world like the pent-up waters behind a dam bursting forth when a dam collapses.

For instance, the mystery of iniquity has long been at work attempting to introduce the antichrist and full-blown apostasy, and God has restrained this effort, preventing the antichrist from being manifested in the world (2 Thess. 2:6-7). But when Jesus opens the first seal, heaven's restraint ends, and the antichrist will ride forth (Rev. 6:1-2) conquering the entire world. This evil man will reveal himself to the world with lying miracles, signs, and wonders wrought with the full power of Satan (2 Thess. 2:9), and he will advance his message with every tool of unrighteous deceit that is available to fallen man (2 Thess. 2:10).

For another example, Satan has devastated mankind for centuries with an orchestrated campaign of stealing, killing, and destroying (John 10:10). Thankfully, this effort has been graciously restrained by God. But when Jesus opens the second, third, and fourth seals, he permits powerful fallen beings to ride forth in a campaign of devastation never seen before on Earth, unhindered by the restraints that have characterized this age. These ungodly angels will be given mind-boggling freedom to wreak havoc through war, famine, plagues, and wild beasts. This cessation of restraint is an act of judgment upon mankind.

What is the aim of the theocratic (kingdom) work that God undertakes during the tribulation? When the Lord takes up the scroll and begins his theocratic work, he has two main aims in sight to be accomplished during the tribulation.

The first is to divide the world into two camps—those who love the light and those who love darkness; those who follow the true Messiah and those who follow the false messiah. There will be no fence riders. The camp of the truth will preach Jesus with an unprecedented presentation of truth and an unprecedented display of supernatural power—the Spirit-baptized Jews, the two witnesses, the hundred and forty-four thousand, and the three angels. The camp of the lie will preach the false messiah with an unprecedented display of lies and deceit and an unprecedented display of supernatural power—giving life to an image of the antichrist, calling down fire from heaven, and working various nefarious miracles and signs.

This divide will be so obvious that no one will accidentally remain in the wrong camp. The platform of the antichrist will be so wrong on so many points of morality and common sense that it will be impossible for any sincere seeker after truth to embrace it. Only an evil heart of unbelief will embrace it. Likewise, the platform of the true Christ will be so passionately committed to the word of God, and so passionately hated and opposed by the world, that it will be impossible for haters of truth to embrace it. Ultimately, this great contest of faith will divide the world into the sheep and goats that we see gathered before the Lord at the second coming in Matthew 25.

The second aim of God's theocratic work during the time of tribulation is to systematically crush everything that men lean on for a crutch: lies, government, military might, political clout, economic strength, education, influence, wealth, fame, power, self-sufficiency, and the like. The desired end is that men might be humbled, turn away from their vain confidence and pride, and look to God in heaven. This destruction is finished at the second coming, when everything left standing is pummeled with mighty stones from above, shaken with an earthquake that rocks the entire globe, and burned with consuming fire from heaven. On that glorious day, when the King of kings descends from heaven, all of man's pride and every symbol of man's pride will be destroyed, and the Lord alone will be glorified (Is. 2:11).

Quantitative Difference

There is also a quantitative difference between the seals and the troubles that have plagued the world during the course of this age. The seals are not the same trials that men have seen with a mere twenty or thirty percent increase, or even a fifty percent increase. The seals are exponentially more severe than anything that mankind has experienced over the past two thousand years.

The fourth seal alone takes twenty-five percent of the world's population. If we assume a population of eight billion, this would be a death toll of two billion people. That is twenty times higher than the death toll for the most devastating war in the history of the world—World War II.

Some challenge this massive number by pointing out that the Bible doesn't actually say that the fallen ones kill one-quarter of Earth's population. It only says that they are given power to kill one-quarter of the world. From this they conclude that the death toll of the fourth seal could be far lower. But this challenge has zero merit. The Bible teaches that the enemy comes to steal, kill, and destroy (John 10:10). This is true not only of Satan himself, but his henchmen too. With such an assessment of the fallen realm coming from God's own lips, there is no chance under the sun that these wretched creatures would fail to exploit this opportunity to the fullest. They are granted permission to kill one-quarter of Earth's population, and they will take full advantage of this opportunity.

The second seal brings a great sword which takes peace from Earth. Notice two things. First of all, this sword takes peace from the entire globe. This has never happened before. While many nations were involved in World War II, the majority were not. Moreover, some of the involved nations experienced little or none of the devastations of war within their own borders. But no nation will be excluded from the ravages of the second seal. The whole globe is involved. Every country in the world will see its cities and infrastructure battered.

Secondly, the sword that impacts every country is a *great* sword. This implies that the nations won't merely suffer some damage. They will experience immense damage. If we assume that, on average, ten percent of the major cities and infrastructure of every nation will be destroyed, that would be a crushing blow to the world. If we further assume that a meagre five percent of the world's population will be killed by this seal, that would come to four hundred million lives, which is four times the death toll of World War II. But my estimates are likely low. The true numbers are probably much higher.

The third seal brings a worldwide famine that devastates mankind. Wars regularly lead to famine. The more severe the war, the more severe the famine. The famine introduced by the third seal will reach the same extreme degree as the wars of the second seal that precipitated it. Since the second seal brought war in a degree and to an extent never before witnessed, so this famine will impact the world in a degree and to an extent never before witnessed. It will be the first global famine in the history of the world.

The fifth seal brings a time of extreme tribulation far beyond anything that has been seen since the beginning of the world. For one thing, it will cover the whole world. Imagine if the persecution that the Jews faced in Nazi-held territory or the persecution that the underground church faces in China or North Korea were worldwide. There would be nowhere to run or hide. There would be no way of escape barring a miracle. The whole world would be a prison camp. That is what it will be like for believers in the tribulation.

For another thing, the persecution in the tribulation will be far worse in its intensity than the world has hitherto witnessed. The Nazi regime and their allies killed an estimated one-third of the Jews in the world. During the tribulation, two-thirds of the Jews will perish (Zech. 13:8-9). This is twice as severe as the persecution of the Jews under Hitler's behest.

The seals must be reckoned as part of the tribulation. In Matthew 24:22 we are informed that the only reason that the tribulation won't result in the extinction of the entire human race is that God has shortened those days. Had he allowed the time to run a little longer, there would be nobody left alive on the planet. This implies that the tribulation involves more than merely the persecution of the saints. It must involve the entire package of visitations at the end of the age, including the seals. When we consider the death and destruction witnessed under the first five seals, we are forced to conclude that it is unreasonable to limit the extinction threat brought by God's tribulation (God's wrath) only to the trumpets and the bowls. The seals by themselves, if they weren't shortened, would bring mankind to utter extinction. Therefore, they are last-days judgment.

The Great Delusion of the Antichrist

Two distinct lines of evidence demonstrate that the antichrist is not merely Satan's wrath against mankind but God's wrath against mankind.

First of all, God himself sends the great delusion of the antichrist to condemn those of hardened heart. With the opening of the first seal (Rev. 6:1-2), God will cease restraining the mystery of iniquity and unleash a strong delusion, centered on the antichrist, that will ultimately engulf the entire planet in the lie (2 Thess. 2:11). The delusion is sent to damn those who rejected the love of the truth (2 Thess. 2:10-12), that is, hardened their hearts against undeniable light. This insight is a theological bombshell. It should settle the issue for all who tremble at the plain statements of scripture. If eternal damnation is judgment, then spiritual delusion sent to bring men to eternal damnation is also a judgment. This means that the antichrist is retributive judgment upon mankind—a manifestation of the wrath of God, albeit manifested in mitigated degree and mingled with grace.

Secondly, God uses ungodly governments and nations to judge his people. For instance, when Judah did not hearken to the prophets and refused to repent of her evil ways, God sent Babylon to judge her (Jer. 25). The nation was crushed, and the inhabitants were left impoverished or carried off into captivity.

In another instance, Israel was commanded to keep herself separate from the Canaanites (Josh. 23). The people were warned that if they engaged in close relationships with the Canaanites and intermarried with them, the Lord would no longer drive them out of the land, but would allow them to become snares and traps and scourges and thorns to Israel, even to the degree that Israel could perish from the promised land. Israel did not heed this warning, and she did indeed suffer the promised judgments.

We could multiply instances from the Bible, but these two examples should suffice to make the point. God has often used ungodly kings and nations to discipline and judge Israel. This is one of the main tools in his toolbox for dealing with his people. In every instance, his wrath and the wrath of man coincided. In the last days, he will once again use ungodly governments to try Israel, sift the nation, and put the godly remnant to flight. First and foremost in this effort will be the antichrist.

Three Lines of Evidence that Seals Are Wrath

We have observed three lines of evidence that clarify the nature of the seals. The first is that the seals are qualitatively distinct from the usual troubles that the world has suffered throughout the age. They feature unrestrained evil as opposed to the restrained evil that mankind has faced throughout the age. The second is that the seals are qualitatively distinct from the usual course of troubles throughout this age. They are vastly worse in their extent and degree than the visitations mankind has faced over the centuries. The third is that the rise of the antichrist is a judgment sent from God to sift Israel and condemn those who have hardened their hearts against the truth.

These lines of evidence demonstrate that it is ad hoc exegesis to claim that the seals are not divine judgment. They are clearly judgment—transcendent visitations appointed for the last times. And if the seals are all judgment, then the promise that the church will be delivered from the wrath to come is a promise that the church will be removed from this planet prior to the opening of the first seal.

PROOF 9

THE RAPTURE AND THE SECOND COMING DISTINGUISHED

One Coming, Two Aspects

Those who believe in a pretribulation rapture are often ridiculed for believing in two comings, a charge which implies that they believe in two second comings. But this accusation is either a mistake or a misrepresentation.

Technically speaking, the pretribulation rapture camp does not believe in or teach two comings. There is only one second coming—the glorious appearance of the Lord Jesus when he descends from heaven to establish his kingdom here on Earth. The rapture is not a distinct coming. It is an aspect of the second coming. What must be understood is that the second coming is the King's glorious entrance and the rapture is the church going out to meet the King prior to his entrance so they can accompany him when he makes his entrance. The distinction between the *glorious coming* and the *going out to meet* will be developed later on in this chapter.

Pragmatically speaking, however, men often speak of two comings in their efforts to distinguish the rapture and the second coming. This is perfectly legitimate. Although the rapture is technically an aspect of the second coming, yet the rapture aspect and the second coming are distinct in time and substance. The former happens *prior to* the tribulation. The latter happens *after* the tribulation. The former is *for* the church. The latter is *with* the church. The former *removes* the church from Earth. The latter *returns* the church to Earth. The *former* goes to heaven. The *latter* brings the kingdom of heaven to Earth.

In the following subsections we will examine six distinctions that prove that the rapture of the church and the second coming are distinct events with a significant amount of time elapsing between them.

Saints Taken vs. Saints Left

The rapture and the second coming are distinct operations that separate mankind in very different ways. In rapture passages we see the saints taken and the ungodly left. In second coming passages we see the ungodly taken and the saints left. Failure to recognize this distinction leads to confusion.

Rapture passages. The removal of the godly is clearly stated in several passages. In 1 Thessalonians 4:13-18, the church is snatched out of the world to meet the Lord in the clouds. In John 14:1-3 the church is taken to heaven when the Lord comes for her. In Revelation 4-5 the church is present in heaven prior to the beginning of the tribulation in Revelation 6. The removal is also implied in various passages. For instance, in Revelation 3:10 we read, "I will keep you from the hour of trial which shall come all the world." This is definitive if you let the words have their natural force. IF the hour of trial comes upon the entire planet, THEN the only way to keep a man from the hour is to remove him from the planet. We go up. The hour of trial comes down.

Second coming passages. The ungodly are taken away at the second coming because they do not meet the sole qualification to enter the promised kingdom—the new birth. Men must be born again to enter the kingdom (John 3:3). We find the removal of the ungodly very clearly stated in the judgment of the sheep and goats (Matt. 25:31-46), where the goats are removed and cast into hell while the sheep are granted entrance into the kingdom. The removal of the ungodly is also clearly stated in the parable of the net, where the bad fish are removed and the good fish are retained (Matt. 13:47-50), and in the parable of the wheat and tares, where the tares are gathered and burned, while the wheat is gathered into the barn (Matt. 13:24-30, 36-43).

The Morning Star vs. the Sunrise

The appearance of the morning star and the rising of the sun are two distinct events that occur at two distinct times in our daily reality. Likewise, the morning star and the sunrise in prophetic typology must be distinct events that occur at distinct times. Denying this undermines biblical typology and implies that much of it lies beyond the pale of discernable meaning.

The morning star is the type that the Lord employs to represent his coming for the church in the last days (2 Pet. 1:19, Rev. 2:28, Rev. 22:16). If the rapture is the morning star of the day of the Lord, then the rapture will happen before the dawning of the day of the Lord.

The dawning of the day is the type that the Lord uses to portray the tribulation (1 Thess. 5, 2 Thess 2). As the dawning of the day overtakes men who are in physical darkness, so the dawning of the day of the Lord will overtake men who are in spiritual darkness. As dawn gradually steals upon men until they realize that the day is upon them, so the dawning of the day of the Lord will gradually steal upon unwary mankind until the truth that the day is here can't be missed or denied.

Notice that the coming of the day upon the world is compared to a woman progressing in labor (1 Thess. 5:3). Her contractions start small and infrequent, then increase in frequency and intensity over time until the moment of birth. So the visitations of the tribulation will increase in frequency and intensity until the birth of the kingdom.

The sunrise of the day is the type the Lord uses to portray the second coming (Mal. 4:1-2, James 1:11), which is the arrival of the day of the Lord in its full intensity and fury. This day brings amazing blessing for the godly and awful judgment for the ungodly. This is the day of Armageddon, the deliverance of Israel, the sheep and goats judgment, the establishment of the kingdom, and the removal of the curse.

The day proper is the type the Lord uses to present the millennium, that is the thousand years. As there are six days of labor and a day of rest according to God's sabbath pattern, so there are six figurative days (6000 years) for the saints to labor in this sewer of unbelief and iniquity and one figurative day (1000 years) for the saints to enjoy God's rest. This pattern is evident when you compare 2 Peter 3:8 (in its context) with the promised rest in Hebrews 4 and the promised third day in Hosea 5:14-6:2. During this time, the Lord alone will be glorified on Earth (Isaiah 2:11).

Now the overall panorama of typology—the rapture of the church portrayed as the morning star, the tribulation portrayed as the dawning of the day, and the second coming pictured as the sunrise or arrival of the day—presents a strong argument for the pretribulation rapture. As the morning star is the first sign of the approaching day, so the rapture is the first sign of the coming day of the Lord. As the morning star precedes the dawning of the day, so the rapture precedes the dawning of the day of the Lord, which time we know as the tribulation.

Going Up vs. Coming Down

One of the critical differences between the rapture and the second coming is that the church will be going up at the rapture and coming down at the second coming. Those who pay close attention to scripture and care about integrity in their handling of scripture will not attempt to force the going up passages and the coming down passages into a single event that happens at one and the same time.

The rapture. The church's upward journey at the rapture has her caught up in the clouds to meet the Lord in the air (1 Thess. 4:16-17). Some grant superficial credence to this passage, yet insist that the rapture is a U-turn journey at the second coming which meets the Lord in the clouds and then descends with him minutes later. But this is an impossible interpretation. According to John 14:1-3, this journey continues to the Father's house in heaven, where the church will dwell with the Lord. We see the same vertical journey with the "Come up here!" (Rev. 4:1) and the subsequent presence of the church in the throne room of God prior to the start of the tribulation (Rev. 4-5). The purpose of the extended stay in heaven is to give the church sufficient time to prepare herself to be the bride of Christ and his coregent over the world (Rev. 19:7). We will be busy training for reigning.

The second coming. When the tribulation comes to an end, the church will make her downward journey, accompanying the Lord in his second coming. The heavens will open, and the Lord will descend on a white horse to engage the antichrist, the kings of Earth, and the armies of the world that have been gathered at

Armageddon (Rev. 19:11-21, Rev. 16:12-16, Ps. 2:1-9). The members of the church will descend with him on their own white horses (Rev. 19:14). The descent of heaven's army is referred to in several other passages in the New Testament (1 Thess. 3:13, Jude 1:14-15) and in the Old Testament (Joel 2:1-12, Is. 13:1-5, Zech. 14:5).

The Bride vs. the Guests

Another clear distinction between the rapture and the second coming is that the former is preceded by the gathering of the bride while the latter is preceded by the gathering of the guests.

In the Epistles and Revelation, the church is pictured as the bride (Eph. 5:25-27, 2 Cor. 11:2, Rev. 19:7-9). Indeed, all who are saved in the present age are part of the bride of Christ. The Lord will come to get his bride and take her to the Father's house before judgment falls on Earth at the end of the age. We call this event the pretribulation rapture.

In the wedding parables in the Gospels, however, we find the believers portrayed as guests at the wedding (Matt. 22:1-14, Matt. 25:1-13). These guests can't be the church. It would be inconsistent for God to refer to the church as both the bride and the guests. So why do we read about guests here? Because these passages have the second coming in view, not the rapture of the church. Indeed, all who are saved during the tribulation will enjoy the privilege of being guests at the church's wedding at the second coming. The principles of salvation and blessing that we see here, however, can be applied to the church.[9]

The scriptures, then, clearly teach that there are two classes of saints at the Lamb's wedding: the bride and the guests. The fact of two classes tells us two things. First of all, there must be a clear line of demarcation which marks the point where the Lord ceases to gather the bride, and he starts to gather the guests. This would be the rapture of the church. Secondly, there must be a sufficiently long period of time after the rapture for the Lord to gather living guests for the wedding. It is natural to associate this gathering time with the seventieth week (the tribulation) as that is when the Lord returns to dealing with Israel to finish his new covenant program with her. When we consider these two points together, they imply that the rapture will happen prior to the tribulation.

Familiar Teaching vs. New Teaching

In his first letter to the church in Thessalonica, Paul paints a rather startling contrast between their comprehension of the day of the Lord (1 Thess. 5:1-11) and their comprehension of the rapture (1 Thess. 4:13-18). They stood in no need of instruction on the former because they were very familiar with the subject— "You have no need that I write to you." But they required instruction on the latter to fill in gaps in their understanding—"I would not have you ignorant, brethren." This implies that the rapture was a new teaching that involved a prophetic event that was distinct from the day of the Lord. Consider the following points.

Familiar teaching. Paul introduced his handling of the day of the Lord in 1 Thessalonians 5:1-11 with this sentence.

> But of the times and seasons, brethren, you have no need that I write to you, for you yourselves know that the day of the Lord comes like a thief in the night.

Why did he preface his treatment in this way? Because the believers were familiar with the subject of the day of the Lord.

They knew, from numerous references in the scriptures and prior ministry, that the dawning of the day of the Lord would catch an unsuspecting world by surprise, that the subsequent visitations would increase in intensity and frequency like a woman's labor pains until the second coming, and that everything still standing on that final day would be burned to ashes or turned to rubble.

Unfamiliar teaching. In 1 Thessalonians 4:13, on the other hand, Paul introduced his rapture teaching with this statement, "I don't want you to be ignorant, brethren." This implies that the subject was relatively new to them, that they didn't have a solid grasp on it, and that the instruction that followed was needed to fill gaps in their prophetic understanding. They knew from earlier instruction on the rapture[10] that living believers would meet the Lord in the clouds (1 Thess. 4:17) and be gathered to the Father's house in New Jerusalem (John 14:1-3). But some aspects of the rapture teaching had eluded them. For instance, they were uncertain about the status of believers who had fallen asleep [died] in Jesus (1 Thess. 4:13). Would they be taken up in the rapture too? Would they go to the heavenly city too? Or was this blessing only for living believers? They also had questions on the circumstances and timing of the rapture, questions which the apostle addressed later in the second letter that he penned to the Thessalonians.

The Thessalonians' fear. The fact that the Thessalonian church feared that Christians who had died might miss out on the rapture is a stand-alone argument that the rapture teaching was new. Here is my line of thinking. The Thessalonians feared that the rapture blessing of a journey to heaven pertained only to the living believers.[11] This fear indicates that they knew that the rapture was not the blessing of the saints at the second coming. Why do I say this? Because they entertained zero doubt about the resurrection of the righteous dead on the last day, a belief held in common by all believers since ancient times (Job 19:26, Dan. 12:1-3, Dan. 12:13, John 11:23-24). They could not possibly have entertained fears about the dead in Christ missing the rapture if they had believed that the rapture was the blessing of the saints at the second coming that they were familiar with.

The mystery of the church. Why did the Thessalonians have gaps in their understanding of the rapture? Because the teaching of the church and her unique place in the last days was new teaching. It had only recently been revealed to the apostles, Paul especially having great insight into the matter (Eph. 3:1-6, Eph. 2:11-16, Rom. 16:25-26). The newness is plainly declared in Ephesians 3:5-6.

> Which in other ages was not made known unto the sons of men, as it is now revealed unto his holy apostles and prophets by the Spirit that the Gentiles should be fellow heirs, of the same body, and partakers of his promise in Christ by the gospel.

Students of the Bible who consistently follow the literal hermeneutic have often observed that we don't see any clear teaching in the Old Testament on the church of this age. Here in Ephesians we have God's confirmation that this observation is true. The church wasn't taught in the pages of the Old Testament. The blessing of the Gentiles had been foretold, but how this would be brought to pass wasn't revealed, except for the simple remark that it would come through the promised seed, that is, through the Messiah (Gen. 22:18).

The first mention of the church in the Bible is the near-horizon prophecy in Matthew 16:18, "Upon this rock I will build my church." At that point, the church didn't exist aside from

God's blueprints. It was still future. It was birthed after the cross at the feast of Pentecost when the promised Holy Spirit was poured out upon the Jewish remnant (Acts 1-2, 1 Cor. 12:12-13). But at that time, the disciples didn't understand fully what was going on. They still saw themselves as a remnant in Israel. Some eight years later, the first Gentiles were grafted in when the Lord sent Peter to visit Cornelius (Acts 10). Not long after, James figured out the existence of God's plan to visit the Gentiles and gather a people for his name (Acts 15). Finally, a few years later, the mystery of the church was revealed (Eph. 2-3), informing the believers that the church was one new man, distinct from Israel, with its own identity, its own path, and its own prophetic destiny.

Contrast with the day of the Lord. The rapture was a new teaching that stood in stark contrast to the day of the Lord. It presented a journey to the glorious courts of heaven above. It was all blessing and no judgment. No aspect of the rapture corresponded with the dawning of the day (the time of bruising judgment on Earth). Nor did any aspect correspond with the arrival of the day (the forceful establishment of the kingdom at the second coming). This contrast with the day of the Lord implies that the rapture will happen before the dawning of the day of the Lord, in other words, before the tribulation.

Conclusion. We examined two distinct arguments that point to the rapture as a new teaching. The first is that the rapture teaching left the Thessalonians confused, contrary to the subject of the day of the Lord with which they were familiar. The second is that the Thessalonians' fears pointed to a distinction between the rapture and the second coming. We also observed that the rapture teaching is pure blessing in contrast to the day of the Lord which is characterized by severe judgment. These three points together imply a pretribulation rapture.

The Parousia vs. the Apantesis

One of the most striking evidences for making a distinction between the rapture and the second coming is found in Paul's well-known rapture passage, 1 Thessalonians 4:13-18. Here, in verses 15-17, Paul draws a distinction between the *parousia* and the *apantesis* of the parousia. The *parousia* is the King's royal entrance (the second coming) and the *apantesis* is his subjects going out to meet him (the rapture) so they can accompany him in his royal entrance. Let's examine this passage and glean the precious truth that it offers on this matter, truth that many readers overlook.

> For this we say unto you by the word of the Lord, that we who are alive and remain until the COMING of the Lord shall not precede those who are asleep. For the Lord himself shall descend from heaven with a shout, with the voice of the archangel, and with the trump of God: and the dead in Christ shall rise first: Then we who are alive and remain shall be caught up together with them in the clouds, to MEET the Lord in the air: and so shall we ever be with the Lord.

Notice the words in small caps. The word *coming* in verse 15 is the Greek word παρουσία (*parousia*). It has a variety of senses along the lines of *coming* and *presence*. The word translated *meet* in verse 17 is the Greek word ἀπάντησις (*apantesis*). It means *meeting* in various nuances. Both of these terms bore technical senses when used for the arrival of kings, a fact which sheds light on the correct understanding of this passage.

Parousia in Koine Greek bore a semi-technical sense when used of a king coming to visit a conquered land or a new emperor entering Rome. (See Deismann's *Light From the Ancient East* and *BDAG[12]*). In such instances it is typically translated *coming*, though *entrance* is a suitable paraphrase because the emphasis is on the moment of arrival. This word is the most common term used in the New Testament for the second coming (e.g. Matt. 24:27, Matt. 24:29-39, 1 Thess. 3:13, 2 Thess. 2:8). Its usage implies the royal entrance of the King of kings.

Apantesis, though often used in a general sense for simple *meeting*, picked up a semi-technical sense when used of loyal subjects going out to meet the approaching king so they could join his train and accompany him in his royal entrance. It wasn't uncommon for folks to make a journey of one or two days to share in this privilege. Theodore of Cyrus described this practice in his handling of this passage in his work *Interpretation of the Fourteen Epistles of Saint Paul*.

> So also with a king entering a city. The most worthy go out to meet him somewhere distant with outlay (personal cost). Those guilty of harboring internal complaints wait for the coming (entrance) of the king.[13]

These semi-technical senses are the senses that *apantesis* and *parousia* bear in 1 Thessalonians 4:15-17. When we grasp this, we will understand this passage in the same way that the average Koine Greek speaker in Paul's day did. We will see a time span between the second coming and the rapture, that is, between the *parousia*, which is the King's royal entrance, and the preceding *apantesis*, which is the church going out to meet their King and join his train so they can accompany him in his royal entrance. This doesn't itself argue for a pretribulation rapture, but it does argue that the rapture must precede the second coming, which strengthens the overall case for a pretribulation rapture.

Glorified Believers vs. Unglorified Believers

The presence of both glorified and unglorified believers in the kingdom is yet another argument that demands a distinction between the rapture and the second coming. The glorified saints will rule with Christ. The unglorified saints will be their subjects in the kingdom of Christ. To flesh this out, we shall examine the three topics that comprise this matter: the glorified church, the reigning church, and the unglorified saints which repopulate the planet during the kingdom.

The glorified church. The Bible teaches that the church will be glorified in the rapture. For example, 1 Corinthians 15:51-53, part of the well-known resurrection passage, states:

> Behold, I show you a mystery. We shall not all sleep, but we shall all be changed in a moment, in the twinkling of an eye, at the last trumpet. For the trumpet shall sound, and the dead shall be raised incorruptible, and we shall be changed. For this corruptible body must put on incorruption, and this mortal body must put on immortality.

Philippians 3:20-21 informs us that this glorification will transform our bodies to be like Christ's glorified body.

> For our citizenship is in heaven, from which we also eagerly wait for the Savior, the Lord Jesus Christ, who will transform our lowly body that it may be conformed to his glorious body.

The church reigning with Christ. The Bible teaches that part of the church's reward will be ruling with Christ. Revelation 2:26-27, for instance, states:

He that overcomes, and keeps my works unto the end, to him will I give power OVER THE NATIONS. And he shall RULE THEM WITH A ROD OF IRON; as the vessels of a potter shall they be broken to shivers, even as I received from my Father.

Numerous other passages present the same privilege from one angle or another (Luke 19:15-27, Rev. 1:6, Rev. 3:21).

The unglorified sheep in the kingdom. If the church is going to reign with Christ in his kingdom, then there must be saints who enter the kingdom in their unglorified bodies and repopulate Earth. The church can't reign if there are no subjects to rule over. We don't rule over each other.

Where do these saints come from? They are the sheep from the sheep and goats judgment when the Lord comes to establish his kingdom (Matt. 25:31-46). The survivors of the tribulation are gathered before the Lord, the sheep (the believers) on his right hand and the goats (the unbelievers) on his left. The goats are slain and cast into hell. The sheep are granted entrance into the kingdom. But the sheep are not glorified. They enter the kingdom in the same bodies that they had in the tribulation. They are able to marry and bear children. Through this remnant, the planet will be repopulated. These believing survivors of the tribulation are also represented in the kingdom parables as good fish (Matt. 13:47-50) and as wheat (Matt. 13:24-30,36-43). They will be a great multitude which no man will be able to number (Rev. 7:9-17).

Now this distinction between the glorified saints and the unglorified saints demands that there be two distinct gatherings of believers in the last days: the gathering of the church at the rapture (the glorified rulers) and the gathering of the living elect at the second coming (the unglorified subjects).

Problem with only one gathering of believers. If there were only one gathering of believers in the last days, and it occurred at the second coming, then there would only be one class of believers, and a literal kingdom would be overthrown.

If you choose the unglorified saints as your only class, you void the resurrection and the kingdom. There would be sheep in unglorified bodies to inherit the kingdom and repopulate Earth, but no glorified believers to reign with Christ over them.

If you choose the glorified church as your only class, you overthrow the kingdom. There would be glorified saints to reign, but no unglorified saints to be ruled over, to inherit Earth, to repopulate Earth. There couldn't actually be a literal, earthly kingdom because all the saints would have heavenly bodies. This is, in fact, the position of amillennialism.

Either option is problematic, indeed fatal, to a literal, earthly, kingdom. We see, then, that upholding a literal kingdom forces us to embrace a distinction between the rapture and the second coming, with enough time between them to secure the salvation of the sheep who will inherit the kingdom. This, for all practical purposes, boils down to a pretribulation rapture.

Seven Distinctions Indicate Pretrib Rapture

We have surveyed seven distinctions that indicate that the rapture and the second coming are distinct events that differ in their timing and their substance: the saints taken vs. the saints left, the morning star vs. the sunrise, the saints going up vs. the saints coming down, the bride vs. the guests, the parousia vs. the apantesis, familiar teaching vs. new teaching, and glorified believers vs. unglorified believers. These points together make a compelling case for a pretribulation rapture.

Proof 10

THE Body and Bride of Christ

Favorite Metaphors

Two of my favorite metaphors in the Bible are the twin descriptions of the church as the body of Christ and the bride of Christ. The truth portrayed by these metaphors is not exhausted with the observation that there is a profound closeness between the Lord and his church. These metaphors are pregnant with far-reaching ramifications in several fields of theology, including eschatology. In this chapter we will examine what they imply about the church's relationship to the tribulation.

The Body of Christ

The Bible teaches that the church is the body of Christ. We read, for instance, in Ephesians 1:22-23:

> [God] has put all things under his feet, and given him to be the head over all things to the church, which is his body, the fulness of him that fills everything in every way.

The truth that the church is the body of Christ implies several things: the Lord and his church are inseparably joined, the Lord shares in the church's pain, the Lord loves the church as himself, and the Lord cannot pour out his end-times judgment on his church. The last point is our focus here, and we will touch on the others only insofar as they have something to say about the church's eschatological deliverance.

It is morally repugnant to think that the wrath of God that is poured out on Earth at the end of the age could be poured out on Christ. How can the eternal Son of God, who spoke the universe into existence, be subject to the wrath of God? If you take the path of substitutionary atonement, he already bore the penalty for the sins of the whole world when he died on the cross as the penal substitute for mankind. He can't pay for man's crimes a second time without double jeopardy. If you take the path of sin, he has neither a criminal record of his own nor a sin nature of his own that must be addressed. When we eliminate these scenarios, we eliminate the only potential scenarios for Christ experiencing the wrath of God. No others exist.

Yet, if it is morally repugnant for wrath to be poured out on Christ, the head of the church, then it just as morally repugnant for wrath to be poured out on the church, the body of Christ. The head and the body can be distinguished, but not divided. The following points shed light on this intimate connection.

Organic unity. The church is described as "one new man" created in Christ himself (Eph. 2:15). Christ is the head of this one new man and the church is the body (Eph. 1:22-23, 5:23, Col. 1:18). When we enter into the depths of this truth, we find that it has eschatological ramifications.

First of all, Christ can not pour out any of the visitations of the last days on his body. If the head and the body are in organic unity, then whatever happens to the body, happens to Christ the head. Were Christ to pour out eschatological judgment while the church was on Earth, that would be morally equivalent to pouring out wrath on himself.

Secondly, if the church is the body and Christ is the head, then the one new man cannot be whole and cannot be present in heaven in its fullness until the body is joined to the head at the rapture. This truth is hinted at in Revelation 12:4-6. And this hint points in the direction of a pretribulation rapture.

> His tail drew a third of the stars of heaven and threw them to Earth. And the dragon stood before the woman who was ready to give birth, to devour her child as soon as it was born. She bore a male child who was to rule all nations with a rod of iron. And her child was caught up to God and his throne. Then the woman fled into the wilderness, where she has a place prepared by God, that they should feed her there one thousand two hundred and sixty days.[14]

If we approach this passage with the understanding that the male child is identical to the one new man, then an amazing pattern can be discerned. The male child (the head) was born in Bethlehem around 2 BC. The male child (the body) was born on Pentecost in AD 33. The male child (the head) will rule the world with a rod of iron because he is the victorious Saviour-Messiah. The male child (the body) will share in ruling the world with a rod of iron (Rev. 2:27). The male child (the head) ascended to heaven ten days before Pentecost[15] in AD 33. The male child (the body) will ascend to heaven at the close of the church age. Note, too, that the head passed the baton to the body in AD 33.

Once we observe this passage through the lens of the one new man, we can better grasp the significance of the *then* in "*then* the woman fled into the wilderness." If the ascension of the male child (the head) is the only thing in view, then there are about two thousand years between the ascension and the woman's flight to the wilderness in the middle of the week. Then the temporal *then* is largely bereft of its usual significance of "at that time." There is no close proximity in time between the Lord's ascent to heaven and the woman fleeing to the wilderness.

But if the ascent of the male child (the body) is also implied, then we invigorate the word *then* with its usual temporal force. Now there are only approximately four years between the male child's ascent and the woman's flight to the wilderness—the first three and a half years of the seventieth week, plus maybe a half year between the rapture and the beginning of the seventieth week. In this instance, the *then* really does mean "at that time."

But this view of the male child does not merely offer a grammatical benefit, it also provides a theological benefit. It points to the close temporal connection between the church going up in the rapture and Israel entering the tribulation. This close connection harmonizes with the fact that the rapture is portrayed in the Bible as the morning star (Rev. 2:28, Rev. 22:16, and 2 Pet. 1:19), while God's return to Israel is portrayed as early dawn (Hos. 6:3, Ps. 46:5). This is yet another hint of a rapture prior to the tribulation.

Positional unity. The connection between Christ and his body is a spiritual reality that far transcends the understanding of many Christians. One of the ways this is communicated is the Bible's teaching on the believer's position in Christ, often called positional truth. This sees the church as already raised and seated in the heavenly realm in Christ Jesus (Eph. 2:6). In the reckoning of God, we have already died and our life is hidden with Christ in God (Col. 3:3). Some day soon—at the rapture—our spiritual position there will be replaced by our physical position there, and the Father will show us the riches of his grace and kindness in Christ Jesus (Eph. 2:6-7).

Now our position in Christ implies a rapture before the tribulation. Because we are already seated with Christ in heaven, we have to be removed from the world before the Lord brings his judgment upon it. It would be just as morally wrong for Christ to pour out judgment on those seated with him in heaven as it would be for him to pour out judgment on those seated with him in his kingdom. If the latter is outrageous, then the former is outrageous. They are cut from the same piece of cloth.

One clarifying thought. Don't confuse judgment in the lesser sense of discipline with judgment in the stricter sense of punitive punishment. They are not the same. The church can experience discipline. "Judgment must begin in the house of God" (1 Pet. 4:17). She can't experience punitive judgment. "He who hears my word and believes in him who sent me has everlasting life and shall not come into judgment" (John 5:24).

Empathetic unity. When the ungodly mistreat the people of God, the Lord takes it personally. For instance, we read in Matthew 25:40, "Inasmuch as you did it unto one of the least of these my brethren, you did it unto me." A similar statement is found in Mark 9:41.

> Whoever shall give you a cup of water to drink in my name, because you belong to Christ, verily I say unto you, he shall not lose his reward.

Matthew 10:42 couches the same thought in terms of the body rather than the head.

> Whoever gives one of these little ones a mere cup of cold water in the name of a disciple, assuredly, I say to you, he shall by no means lose his reward.

Now this principle of empathetic unity enhances the other body-based arguments that imply the necessity of a rapture before the tribulation. Positional unity says, "I will impute whatever is done to the body as having been done to the head." Organic unity says, "Whatever is done to the body is done to the whole." Empathetic unity says, "Whatever is done to the body, I (the head) take it personally, and I will respond with all the jealousy that heaven can muster."

These arguments present a strong case that the church cannot see any of the visitations of the seventieth week. Bear in mind that all judgment on Earth and in heaven has been given to Christ. He is the administrator of the judgments of the last days. The administrator will certainly ensure that none of these judgments fall on himself, the head. But he has a further obligation. He can no more allow these judgments to fall on his body than he can allow them to fall on himself, the head. Those dear saints who are organically connected to him, positionally placed in him and seated with him, and empathetically defended by him cannot see any of the judgments of the seventieth week. They must, by dint of their connection with him, meet the Lord in the clouds before the seventieth week begins.

The Bride of Christ

The fact that the church is the bride of Christ presents two distinct arguments for a pretribulation rapture.

The one-flesh argument. The Bible states that the husband and wife are one flesh (Eph. 5:31). When the husband loves his wife, he loves himself (v. 28). She is his flesh (v. 29). The Bible further presents earthly marriage as a picture of the relationship between Christ and the church (v. 32). The church is the bride of Christ, loved and nourished by Christ her husband (v. 29). She is his flesh and bones (v. 30). They are one flesh (v. 31).

This precious truth presents a strong argument for a rapture before the tribulation. Because the church is the bride of Christ, the Lord cannot allow his end-times judgments to fall upon the church. Allowing the bride to go through this time of awful visitation is contrary to loving your wife as yourself. Why would a man keep himself out of this time of judgment, and yet allow— or worse, require—his wife to endure it? That makes no sense.

The wedding supper argument. Several facets of this picture demand our attention, which when considered together point to a pretribulation rapture.

First of all, the public feast of the wedding takes place at the second coming. This we understand from Revelation 19:6-9 when we consider its context, which is the second coming.

> Halleluia! For the Lord God Almighty has begun to reign. Let us be glad, rejoice, and give honour to him, for the marriage [supper] of the Lamb has come, and his wife has made herself ready. And to her was granted that she should be arrayed in fine linen, clean and white, for the fine line is the righteousnesses of the saints. And he said to me, write, Blessed are those who are invited to the marriage supper of the Lamb.

Locating the wedding supper at the second coming stands to reason when you consider the big picture of God's redemption plan. For one thing, it allows all of the saved of all of the ages to be present at the festivities. None are left out. If the wedding supper were to take place in heaven shortly after the rapture, then none of the living tribulation saints would be able to attend. This seems wrong. For another thing, it allows all of the saints who are destined for the resurrection to attend the wedding in their glorified bodies. None are left out. If the wedding supper were to take place in heaven shortly after the rapture, then the Old Testament saints and the tribulation martyrs would have to attend the glorified bride's wedding supper without their own resurrection bodies. This seems awkward and unreasonable.

Another argument for locating the wedding supper at the second coming is found in the wedding account in Matthew 22, where we read about a guest who showed up at the wedding feast without a wedding garment (Matt. 22:11-12). He was bound and cast into outer darkness. This is impossible to reconcile with a wedding supper in heaven shortly after the rapture. How can an unsaved man show up in heaven? Does the Lord rapture one ungodly person just to make the point? This situation absolutely demands that the wedding supper occur at the second coming.

Secondly, when the bride descends from heaven for the wedding supper, she has been in heaven for a while making herself ready (Rev. 19:7). This implies a significant length of time between the rapture and the second coming. Note, too, that the army which descends wearing white linen (Rev. 19:14) is the bride in white linen mentioned earlier (Rev. 19:7). The descent of the bride for the wedding is one and the same as the descent of the army for Armageddon. Both man and beast will feast on that day. The wild beasts will feast on the flesh of the fallen ungodly while the godly will feast on the amazing dishes that will be served at the wedding supper.

Thirdly, the wedding parables in the Gospels portray the gathering of wedding guests (Matt. 22:1-14, Matt. 25:1-13). This is significant. Currently, the gospel is gathering the bride for the wedding. After the rapture, the gospel will gather guests for the wedding supper that takes place at the second coming. When does the switch take place? There is only one logical location. Prior to the seventieth week. The Lord has declared seventy weeks upon the people and nation of Israel (Dan. 9:24-27). This implies that the Lord will switch from his church program to his Israel program—from gathering the bride to gathering the guests—before the seventieth week. So there will be seven years plus a short window of time for the gospel to gather guests for the wedding.

Let's now consider all three pieces of the wedding supper revelation together. First, the wedding supper will be celebrated at the second coming. Second, the bride will have spent time in heaven before the second coming making herself ready for her position as the bride of Christ. Third, the guests for the wedding will be gathered before and during the seventieth week that the Lord declared upon Israel and Jerusalem. When we put these pieces together, they point to the bride spending seven-plus years in heaven prior to the wedding supper at the second coming. This is a pretribulation rapture.

Twin Truths Demand Pretrib Rapture

We understand from the New Testament that the church is—on the spiritual plane—the body of Christ. He is the head, and the church is his body. Together they comprise one new man. We further gather from the New Testament that the church is—on the spiritual plane—the bride of Christ. As the husband and wife become one body and one flesh, so Christ and his bride will become one body and one flesh. Indeed, earthly marriage is intended to be a picture of the heavenly marriage between Christ and his bride (Eph. 5:32).

Once we enter into the profound depths of these twin truths, we are forced to conclude that the church cannot go through the time of tribulation. The Lord cannot bring end-times judgment upon the planet until the head and the body are joined together in heaven, otherwise he would be bringing judgment upon himself. The Lord cannot take up his theocratic work and begin to exercise his role as King of kings here on Earth until his bride is at his side, in heaven. If he allows or requires his bride to ride out the time of judgment while he watches from the outside, he runs afoul of the command to love his wife as himself, and he breaches the truth that they are one flesh.

CONCLUSION

In this volume I have provided ten distinct arguments which definitively prove the pretribulation rapture. These arguments demolish the common soundbite, "There is no evidence in the Bible for a pretribulation rapture!" The fact is, the evidence in the Bible for the church's departure prior to the tribulation is overwhelming. Only a spirit of error that exalts theories over a robust and consistent application of the historical-grammatical hermeneutic will resist this evidence.

But there is a reason for this resistance to truth. Strong winds of change—winds of departure—are howling with gale-force blasts. Evangelicals are being blown and tossed by theories galore that assail the Bible, the church, Israel, the Jews, and the literal interpretation of prophecy. The entire prophetic revelation of God in the word of God is under attack. The pretribulation rapture of the church, in particular, is in the crosshairs of this storm of unbelief. May God help us to withstand these winds. May we plant our feet firmly on the word of God and the hope set before us.

Keep looking up! Soon this battle will be over, and we will be going home!

Eyes wide open, brain engaged, heart on fire!
Lee Brainard

ENDNOTES

[1] The Hebrew of Daniel 9:27 and most of the English translations say "the many," which means "the most" or "the majority."

[2] The warning to flee Judea is a warning to flee Israel. Judea was the name of the nation where the descendants of Jacob lived in the time of Christ. Israel is the name of the nation where the descendants of Jacob live in our era, though the borders of modern Israel significantly surpass those of Judea in the time of Christ.

[3] To go deeper into this subject, see *The Meaning of "Earth Dwellers" and the Book of Revelation* by Thomas D. Ice, a research paper published by Liberty University. It can be accessed on the Pre-Trib Research Center website and in Liberty University's expansive digital resources collection at https://digitalcommons.liberty.edu/cgi/viewcontent.cgi?article=1045&context=pretrib_arch.

[4] I spent many hours examining the use of the Greek verb tēreō in Koine works and found five instances of tēreō ek. All expressed the sense of *preservation from* as opposed to *preservation in*. For instance:

Josephus, *Antiquities of the Jews*, 5.26, "He commanded them also to bring together all the silver and gold, **preserved from** the city that they first took, that it might be set apart as first-fruits unto God." This refers to the destruction of Jericho. The gold and silver were removed from the city for safekeeping, then everything else was destroyed.

Ephraim, *Ethical Sermons to the Monks of Egypt*, Oration 16, "Rigorously **keep yourself from** forwardness, lest you become enslaved to talking too much and shamelessness." He is not advising believers to keep themselves while engaging in forwardness but to avoid it altogether.

Origen, *Exposition in Proverbs*, Migne 17.196, "He that keeps them [the commands of God], **keeps** his soul **from** death." He is not claiming that those who keep the commands of God protect their souls while in death, but that they keep them from death.

It is also noteworthy that the Greek language had a tēreō form that they used when expressing the preservation of something in a trial—the verb diatēreō. Here are three examples:

Ephraim, *Sermon on the Advent, the End of the Age, and the Antichrist*, Phrantzolas, 4.114. "For many shall be found at that time ... in the mountains and in the desert places ... The Holy God ... shall **preserve** them—they shall

115

be hidden there." Ephraim opines that the Lord will preserve the tribulation saints, saved by the ministry of the two witnesses, through the tribulation.

Athanasius, *History of the Arians*, ch. 24. "May Divine Providence **preserve** you, my dearly beloved parent, through many years." His parent was preserved or kept through the years.

Plutarch, *Lives*, Pericles, 39.1. "So, then, the man is to be admired not only for the reasonableness and meekness which he **preserved** in the midst of many endeavors and great enmities, but also for his loftiness of spirit." This is preserving (keeping) one's character in the midst of trials.

[5] The verse, "The Lord knows how to deliver the godly from a TRIAL and reserve the unjust for punishment in the day of JUDGMENT," is a classic example of Hebrew parallelism in the New Testament. Sometimes the two lines give the same thought in different words, sometimes they provide two pieces of information on the same situation. The latter is the case here. The two lines address the fate of the godly and the ungodly in the same situation.

[6] J.N. Darby was an accomplished Greek scholar, able to read Classical and Koine Greek as well as the Greek New Testament. It was his fluency in Greek that helped him to grasp the true force of this passage. He wrote, "It is true that huper in certain cases signifies 'as concerning'; that is, that it is almost the sense of peri. But it is unquestionable that when it is employed with words of prayer request, its regular meaning in Greek is 'by,' 'for the sake of.' No person who is at all familiar with the Greek tongue, or who is willing to take the trouble of using a good dictionary, would deny it … It is this passage which, twenty years ago, made me understand the rapture of the saints before—perhaps a considerable time before—the day of the Lord (that is, before the judgment of the living)." [*The Collected Writings of J.N. Darby*, Vol. 11, p. 67.]

[7] The verb here, ἐνέστηκεν (enestēken), the perfect tense of ἐνίστημι (enistēmi), means *be among, be present*. It is translated *at hand* in the KJV, *had come* in the NKJV, *has come* in the NASB and ESV, and *is present* in Darby. The best translation here is *is present*. The translation *at hand* is tolerable if you understand *on the door step* rather than *on the horizon*. The translations *had come* (the pluperfect), *has come* (past perfect), and *is come* (present perfect) are also workable as they offer essentially the same idea as *is present*, merely approaching the subject from a different angle. But they do not have the visceral force of *is present*.

One of the strongest proofs that the core sense really is *is present* is that the Koine Greeks called the present tense ο ενεστως Χρονος (ho enestōs chronos), the present time. See A.T Robertson's remarks on p. 350 of *A Grammar of the Greek New Testament in the Light of Historical Research*, Broadman Press, 1934.

116

[8] The commentaries are full of half-baked reasons why ὑπέρ (huper) here must be translated as if it were περί (peri). One of the common reasons offered is that the passage makes no sense when you translate it as a formula jurandi (a formula of swearing)—e.g. by Jove, by God—which a man employs when he vows to do something. But this is a straw man. Pretribulationist do not argue for a formula jurandi here. On the contrary, they argue for a standard petition in its full form: a request for something that includes the reason for the request.

[9] While these passages are second coming passages, we can legitimately apply the salvation and blessing principles to the saints of the present age (the church age) because the generic principles are non-dispensational. They apply to all the saints of all the ages.

[10] Paul had spent a month or two with the church in Thessalonica and had covered the rapture. But the Thessalonians still had questions on the subject as we discern from both 1 Thessalonians 4 and 2 Thessalonians 2.

[11] The Thessalonians appear to have feared that only the living saints would participate in the rapture blessing and experience the glories of heaven. The sleeping saints would have to wait until the second coming to receive their blessing, and that would only include the resurrection and the earthly kingdom. They would entirely miss out on the glories of New Jerusalem.

[12] BDAG is the abbreviation for A Greek-English Lexicon of the New Testament and Other Early Christian Literature, being a translation of Walter Bauer's Griechisch-Deutsches Wörterbuch zu den Schriften des Neuen Testaments und der übrigen urchristlichen Literatur, executed by Frederick Danker, William Arndt, and Wilbur Gingrich.

[13] Theodore of Cyrus, Interpretatio in xiv epistulas sancti Pauli, Migne, vol 82, p 649. The original runs, Οὕτω καὶ βασιλέως εἴς τινα πόλιν εἰσιόντος, οἱ μὲν ἐν τέλει καὶ ἀξιώτατοι πόρρω που ἀπαντῶσιν·οἱ δὲ ἐγκλήμασιν ὑπεύθυνοι ἔνδον προσμένουσι τὴν τοῦ κριτοῦ παρουσίαν.

[14] This passage is a chiasmus. The ends (v. 4a and v. 6) address the middle of the seventieth week. The front end addresses Satan being cast to Earth at the midpoint of the tribulation and taking one-third of the angels with him. The back end addresses the flight of believing Israel to the wilderness for preservation which happens at the same time. The inner portion concerns the birth of Christ and his ascension, which mark the start and finish of his earthly ministry. In v. 5a we find the birth of Christ. In v. 4b we find Satan's efforts to destroy the Messiah as soon as he was born, which took place in the days of Herod when he commanded all the children under two to be executed. In 5b we find the child ascended to heaven.

[15] Note that the head of the church was raptured to heaven forty days after First Fruits and ten days prior to Pentecost—off the Jewish calendar. This implies that the body of the church will be raptured off the Jewish calendar.